OUT OF THE WOODS

From Deerfield to the Grand Circuit

ELLEN WILLIAMS

Palmetto Publishing Group
Charleston, SC

Out of the Woods
Copyright © 2019 by Ellen Williams

First Edition

Printed in the United States

ISBN-13: 9-781-64111-359-5
ISBN-10: 1-64111-359-6

ACKNOWLEDGMENTS

The author wishes to thank the following, without whose help this project would not have been possible: Barbara Robbins Cobb, Eugene A. Seelye, W. David Kilburn, Roberta Bouche, Earle D. Robbins, and Maryon Painter Swanson, for the sharing of photos and memorabilia. For family oral history, Mary Wood Wetmore, John R. Wood, and the late Eleanor Chapin Robbins. For previous genealogical groundwork, Mark Wood. The following organizations housed archives and collections significant to this project, and appreciation is extended to the following individuals who shared items from those collections: Paul Wilder at the Harness Racing Museum and Hall of Fame, Robert Lowell Goller at the Town of East Aurora History Office, Kirk House at the Steuben County Historical Society, Denise Golden at the Bradford County Historical Society, Cynthia VanNess at the Buffalo History Museum, and Rachel Dworkin at the Chemung County Historical Society. The Green Free Library in Wellsboro and the Knoxville Public Library also held valuable research materials. Thanks to Hilma Cooper and Eugene A. Seelye for reading early drafts and giving suggestions. Thank you to my patient husband for the peculiar road trips along the way.

TABLE OF CONTENTS

INTRODUCTION

You will never forget stories told to you by your grand old folk,
and you, like me, may be reluctant to dig into the cold facts
for so often dreams are a better reality.
But you must you know, for Grandfather may not have told half the story
and that untold story may be the best part of all. [1]

As America's sense of identity came into focus and roads across the trackless wilderness connected the frontier with the growing cities, the need for faster and smoother transportation drove the development of the trotting horse. The Civil War put a temporary hold on that pursuit, but the optimism in the North after the war bubbled into progress that could not be contained. The building of better roads allowed for the fun and function of a light road horse. While first canals and then railroads moved freight, horses hauled the daily mail coach or the family to church. The urge to get everywhere faster was a pastime common folks could enjoy, and the building of tracks and racing clubs soon followed.

New York, Long Island, and the Hudson River region made up the core of trotting enthusiasm prior to the Civil War, and most of

---

1 Bertram H. Groene, *Tracing Your Civil War Ancestor*, (Winston-Salem, North Carolina, John H. Blair, Publishers, 1973), 91-92.

the sires of fast driving horses originated from this area. Yet in 1861, a farmer named Oliver L. Wood (+/-1800–1882) migrated from his home in Orange County, New York, to the sparsely-settled lumber territory of northern Pennsylvania. He brought with him a two-year-old colt he called Dan. The colt had been bred from the line of William Rysdyk's Hambletonian, the biggest name in Orange County. Wood was a dairy farmer, but he did not race horses. He likely had no idea that the colt would become one of the most well-known residents of his new Tioga County home within a short while. Over his lifetime of almost thirty years, spent at Wood's farm outside the small village of Knoxville, the horse became known as Wood's Hambletonian and sired some of the most well-known harness track performers to come from Pennsylvania.

When the persistent legend of the stallion spurred the author of this book to track down the story, only a handful of clues remained. It seemed a cold trail: more than 150 years had passed since Wood arrived in Tioga County from Orange County with his colt. An oil painting of Wood's Hambletonian hung in the local public library. A small black-and-white photo, from which the painting had been made, was displayed there also with a breeding card advertisement dated 1882. The older members of the Wood family were certain of a few facts: the horse's name, the year Wood brought him from New York in 1861, and that the horse was very famous. They also knew that the stallion was a roan, a mixture of tones from deep brown to light gray, giving the horse a speckled or dappled coat. Details beyond that had died with the previous generation of Woods. Memories of tractors on the farm were crystal clear, but the horses were long gone.

Across the span of a century and a half, primary sources like diaries, photographs, farm ledgers, legal records, censuses, and vintage news archives revealed a very different language of culture. When Oliver L. Wood was attracted to Tioga County, the young nation was full of optimism on the wave of the Industrial Revolution. Timber and farming opportunities beckoned many ever farther west. The Woods were not wealthy and as farmers they stayed in the Cowanesque Valley, hours away from any city. The stallion was transferred from father to sons and became the window to a larger world: the premier national sporting pastime of the Gilded Age. Everyone from hucksters to congressmen wanted a piece of the trotting action, and the Wood horse provided that in the rural region along the northern border of Pennsylvania.

There was not much competition to the sport; no baseball league, no NFL, and NASCAR was in the distant future. Wood's Hambletonian #572, as he was officially named, sired fast horses who drew wealthy folks to the hinterlands of Pennsylvania's lumber region. Sometimes the Woods ventured further afield to follow the sport. The horse, also known as Old Dan, turned up frequently in stock and racing journals for years after his death, as his speed and distinctive coloring carried through his racing offspring around the nation.

This narrative documents the stories of seven of the stallion's offspring that range across his life-span, from earliest to latest. Their racing careers are chronicled along with anecdotes and adventures of their owners, drivers, and rivals on the track. Stories of horses who stayed in Tioga County serve as corollaries to the main seven. The social history of the Wood family and the local region includes other local horsemen and events upon which life in that era turned. It provides a glimpse into a time long gone, when horse power and horse sport tied this outlying region to the mainstream pulse of a nation riding the high tide of the Industrial Revolution.

These are the seven horses:

Kilburn Jim (1866–1872)

Nancy Hackett (1870—1879)

Minnequa Maid (1874–?) + Nightingale (1885–1896)

Scapegoat (1892–1913)

Mamie Wood (1884–?) + Skyland Girl (1892–?)

Supporting stories include those of Argonaut, full brother to Nancy Hackett, Regina, full sister to Mamie Wood, Blue Mare, Allegany Boy, Elda B., and others who propel the narrative up to 1920. The achievements of the pacing mare Skeeter W. and the Canadian Horse Racing Hall of Fame stallion Chilcoot bring the tale full circle. An appendix will include a listing of horses descended from Wood's Hambletonian with their location and achievements where found.

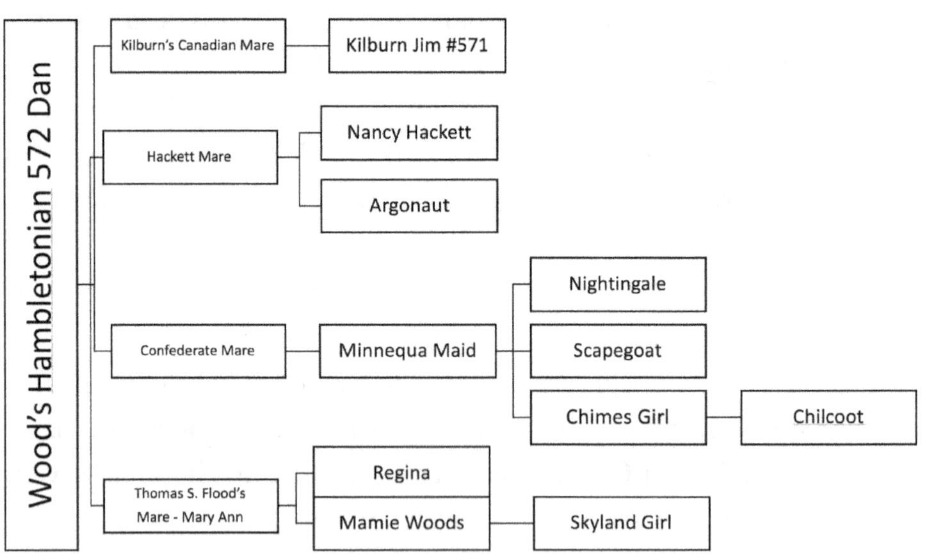

HORSES IN THIS NARRATIVE DESCENDED FROM WOOD'S HAMBLETONIAN.

CHAPTER 1

HOW THE WOOD FAMILY CAME TO DEERFIELD

Oliver L. Wood was a farmer past sixty years of age in 1861 when he decided to pull up stakes in Minisink, Orange County, New York. Young folks left home on a whim, but their roots were not embedded so deeply. It took a strong force to impel an aging couple to leave their farm and familiar life and move to northern Pennsylvania. The region was then only partially cleared of timber, with pockets of farmland not yet accessible by railroad. But Oliver and his wife, Thankful (née Everitt), were not the first of their family to move to the region.

The Woods already had relatives in the Pennsylvania region, and their two older sons, Absalom Simmons Wood and Oliver Hezekiah (known as O. H.) Wood, had bought farmland north of Knoxville during the 1850s. When Oliver and Thankful's youngest son, Joseph—born in 1846—was old enough to do heavier farm work as a young teenager, they sent him to Deerfield to live with and help his older brother, Absalom, on his farm. Absalom had no sons.

ABSALOM SIMMONS WOOD, AKA ABSALOM SIMEON WOOD. (COURTESY BARBARA ROBBINS COBB.)

About a year later, in 1861, the Wood parents packed up their household. Loading furniture and tools into wagons and driving their livestock, they journeyed to Deerfield themselves that spring. Because dairy cows were part of their livestock, it was clear that Oliver intended to produce milk and butter to sell in addition to the other diversified farm products of the time. What was not clear was what his intentions were for the nice, pedigreed colt he brought along. Why would an aging dairy farmer whose main income was from butter sales to nearby New York City move his home to a remote region known mostly for lumber, without a rail connection, and bring along a racehorse?

With Oliver and Thankful came another son yet unmarried, William C., age twenty-six. A closer look at the family of Oliver and Thankful in 1861 provided context: The oldest son, Absalom Simmons Wood, was thirty-eight years old and married, with one daughter. He raised dairy cattle at his place just north of Knoxville on the Austinburg road. The second son and most avid horseman, O. H., was thirty-four years old, married with a son thirteen years old and two younger children. O. H. owned tracts of land north and west of Knoxville, having bought and sold various timber tracts and farms in the area before the arrival of his parents.

Wood's third child, a daughter, Phebe Jane, was age thirty-three. She had put down roots with her husband, Elias Perry Masterson, a photographer with a thriving studio in Port Jervis, New Jersey, just across the state line from Unionville. Eventually her sister, Mary, age twenty-eight, would follow with her husband, Martin Wilson, to live near Knoxville as well.[1] Another grown son, Thomas E. Wood,

---

1 F. J. Wood, "Sketch of Life of Oliver Livingston Wood" (unpublished manuscript, March 24, 1965), private collection of Mary Wood Wetmore.

age twenty-two, was learning photography skills in Port Jervis under his brother-in-law Masterson.

In 1861, the family was at a juncture; some were staying, some had already left. For the 1860 census in Minisink, their third daughter, Emily Wood, was age seventeen still living with her parents.[2] But she was being courted by a young farmer who was well established there, Samuel Christie. With their wedding approaching, Thankful may have been hesitant to leave until she saw Emily settled. Although weddings were simple, small affairs, the culture mandated some preparation. The bride and her mother would sew a new wardrobe and household linens to bring to the new marriage. At the time those were items folks did not have the means to purchase; things were hand-sewn in generous quantities to last the new wife for some time into the future and included the expected birth of children.

If the Wood men were anxious to get to their new home, oral tradition hinted that Thankful was less than enthusiastic about departing for new territory.[3] She may have dug in her heels, to stay at least until her youngest daughter was properly married. Thankful had borne ten children, eight grew to adulthood, and of those only two daughters remained in the old home: Phebe Masterson and Emily Christie. Of the couple's sons, three would become horsemen in the family: O. H., William C., and the youngest, Joseph.

Several families connected to the Woods migrated to Knoxville and nearby townships around this time: Wainwrights, Everitts, Coles, Cases, and Simmonses were also in both locales. These families were linked to the Woods in a myriad of ways: by birth, by marriage, and

---

2 US Census, State of New York, County of Orange, Town of Minisink, 1860. HeritageQuest Online.

3 Maryon Painter Swanson, conversation with the author, 2018.

livelihood. The lure of fertile, cheap farmland and lumber opportunities beckoned many during that decade. The Woods were not among the first wave of settlers to come to Deerfield. The main acreage they came to occupy was previously the home of the Cloos family.

It was that clan who first came to the rich river bottom of the Cowanesque when it was opened for settlement shortly after 1800. It was Clooses who cleared the hemlock and pine, cultivated the first crops, and built the simple frame houses and barns on the place. In the second generation, a subsequent Cloos farmer mortgaged the farm to Joel Parkhurst of Elkland. When he died the mortgage fell into default. Parkhurst took back the deed for the farm, which contained about 220 acres, and found another farmer—Oliver L. Wood—who would assume the payments.[4] Likely one of Oliver's sons or other relatives wrote to him in Unionville when they got wind that the Cloos farm was available.

"The Cowanesque River has its source in Potter County and flows eastwardly just south of the state line to its confluence with the Tioga at Lawrenceville. The valley through which it passes is one of surpassing beauty and by far the richest and most productive district in the county."[5]

---

4 Tioga County Deed Book 35, 310.
5 John F. Meginness, *History of Tioga County, Pennsylvania* (Philadelphia: R. C. Brown, 1897), 27.

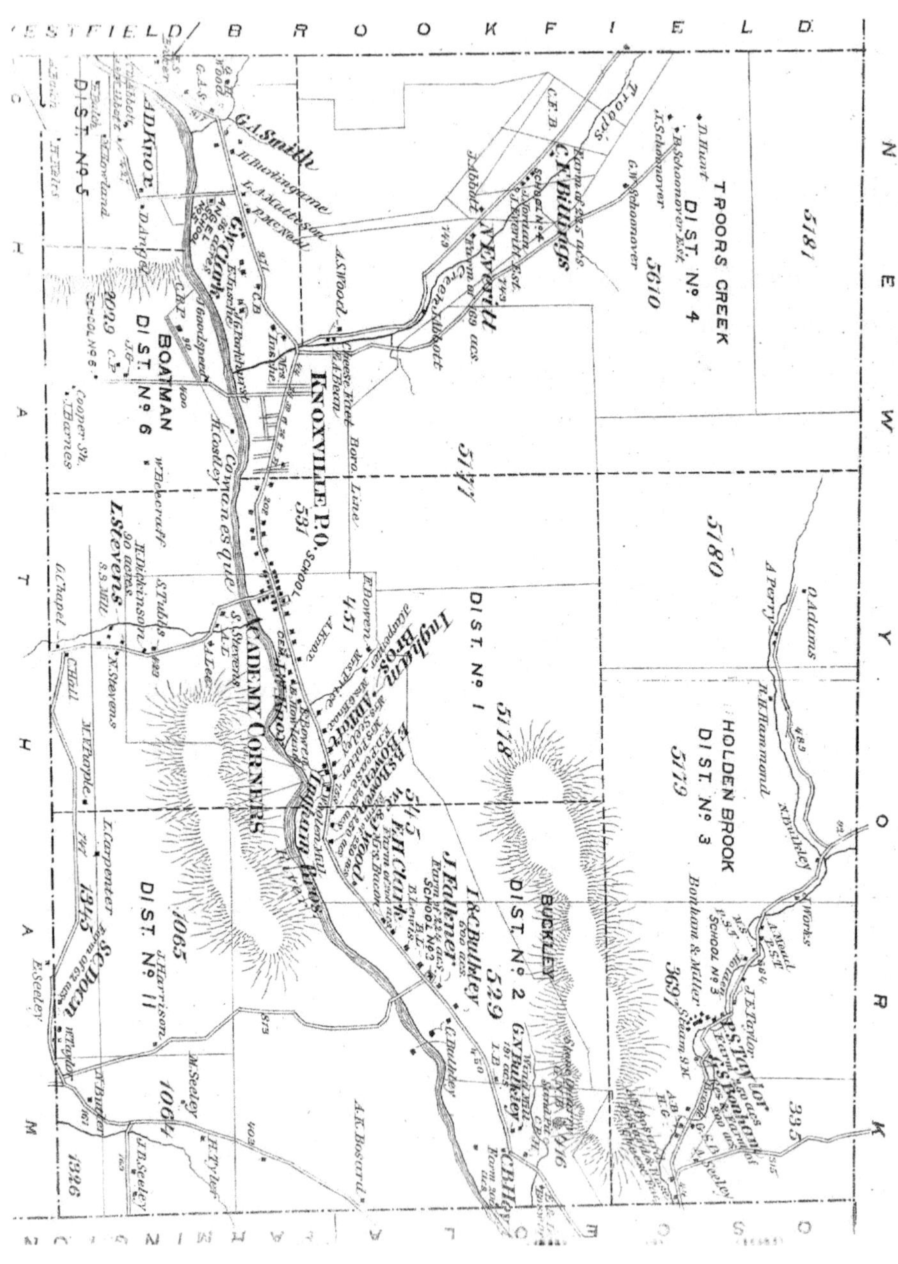

DEERFIELD TOWNSHIP IN 1875.[6]

6 *Atlas of Tioga County, Pennsylvania* (New York: F. W. Beers, 1875), 23.

Two situations begged for context at the onset of the Civil War. First, the money question: How were Woods doing business? There was no structured bank in Knoxville during the 1860s and early 1870s, and since a barter economy prevailed, people did not require cash for food or commodities often. When they needed cash, they borrowed it from friends or family. This kinfolk banking system of unsecured notes was the equivalent of today's ATM transactions. There were individuals who operated like a bank, such as Joel Parkhurst in Elkland. Charles and David Billings, Knoxville sons of the lumber baron Silas Billings, also lent cash.

Loans like this were often unsecured and made for interest rates at 10–12 percent, particularly after the financial panic of 1873. The notes payable then became liquid assets, which people traded, assigned, or sold to others. Then the current owner of the note, who might be unknown to the borrower, might knock at the door and request payment according to the terms of the note.[7] Woods were doing this often, and how much of this was to finance horses wasn't known. However, it was clear that O. H. Wood was right in the thick of this with his own son, father, and brothers during the peak horse years.[8]

By the late 1870s, there were several private banks in Tioga County, such as Joel Parkhurst's bank in Elkland. Parkhurst had his fingers into everything, and at various points he owned the hotel in Knoxville, later to be known as the Adams House where the Citizens & Northern Bank now is located. He even owned the Penn Wells Hotel in Wellsboro for a short time in the 1870s. C. L. Pattison was the son-in-law of Joel Parkhurst and assumed the business,

---

7 Robert M. Sandow, *Deserter Country* (Fordham University Press, 2009), 24.

8 *Wood v. Billings*, 166 Sup. Ct. M. D. Pa. (May Term 1881)

later known as Pattison National Bank.[9] In the northern part of the county were more privately held options, like Morgan Seely's bank in Osceola, Perry Tucker's bank in Knoxville, or the Wickham & Aiken bank in Tioga discussed in an upcoming chapter.

Second, the soldier question: When the Civil War was on, why didn't any of the Wood men go? The Woods would have arrived in Tioga County in the spring early enough to get crops planted, but whether it was before Fort Sumter wasn't known. None of them enlisted when Lincoln first called for volunteers, nor was there evidence that any of them served after the 1863 draft, although with the exception of father Oliver L. and Joseph at age 15, they were all eligible. Only O. H. was mentioned in connection with the draft as "failed to report" in March of 1865, as not having the teeth required to bite off cartridge caps.[10]

The Deerfield township clerk at the time recorded that the quotas in 1863 through 1864 were filled each time either by paid substitutes or bounty. The bounties were higher just across the state line in New York, yet no evidence was found that any Woods went with a regiment from there either. In a time when most other families had one or often several men off to fight, it was a question worth pondering.[11] Several of their obituaries indicated that the Wood men—and at least some of their Everitt kin—were staunch Democrats. Though the derisive terms "Peace Democrat" or "Copperhead" used to describe antiwar folks became prevalent only later as the war dragged on, the Woods' political leanings may have made them a minority in their new neighborhood. As newcomers to Deerfield, they may not

---

9 Elkland Centennial, 1850–1950.

10 John Sexton, *History of Tioga County, Pennsylvania, with Illustrations, Portraits, and Sketches, etc.* (New York: W. W. Munsell, Press of George MacNamara, 1883), 321.

11 Ibid., 237.

have felt peer pressure as keenly because they had not yet formed attachments with the families who were sending sons and husbands off to fight.

Regardless of these uncertainties, one fact is clear: Orange County in the Hudson Valley was called the Cradle of the Trotter for good reason. The town of Chester was where Jonas Seely's mare gave birth to Hambletonian, the colt who would make his mark in the world as Rysdyk's Hambletonian #10. That single stallion would pass on the fast, smooth trotting gait as a dominant trait to his many offspring and would be the name on which the new, uniquely American horse breed would be built.

The farmers in that region had flourished with their mode of agriculture. Diversified farms sustained their families with milking herds of Jersey, Alderney, or Ayrshire cows. Many made butter on their farms or took milk to the plentiful nearby creameries. Creameries in Unionville could ship high-quality butter by rail promptly into the city of New York and get premium prices. In the days when butter was the gold standard of nutrition, Orange County butter had a reputation for being the best there was.

Rysdyk's Hambletonian was a game-changer for agriculture in Orange County:

> The brilliant performances of his colts upon the turf had now given their sire a national reputation. They were in great demand, and commanded high, and in many instances, exorbitant prices; and the breeding of trotters received a new and greater impetus than ever before throughout the county. A new road to fortune and wealth was opened, and many a farmer, into whose brain the idea of making a dollar in any other

way than by the production of milk and butter had
never entered, prompted by the success of a neighbor,
turned his attention to breeding horses . . .[12]

For the pedigree of Rysdyk's horse, see the plentiful online resources available.

Because an overland journey behind a galloping stage-coach
team was so rough it left one feeling beat up, an animal that could
maintain a smooth gait at high speed was a desired improvement.
The 2.5-minute mile time was what the evolving harness-horse
sporting circles would settle on as their "standard" necessary to register a horse into the new breed record books: they would call it the
Standardbred horse. For the first time, a group of horses was select-
ed on performance rather than pedigree or appearance. The horses
were crossbreds, mixing Thoroughbred bloodlines with Morgan,
Narragansett (two other uniquely American types at that time), and
Arab strains. The resulting fast horses trotted or paced smoothly,
could keep up the gait over long road distances, and transmitted
those natural qualities to their offspring as a dominant trait. In the
southern states where riding horses prevailed, breeds such as the
Tennessee Walker and Missouri Fox Trotter developed during the
same era.

Oliver Wood's farm was in Minisink, and his neighbors throughout Chester, Wantage, and Warwick were breeding and racing
trotting horses with a fervor equal to the enthusiasm of the young
nation. Then as now, you were a product of your local culture and
you did what your peers were doing. Men like Alden Goldsmith,
Israel Tuthill, and Jonas Seely were all into racehorses up to their

---

12   Reeves, *Orange County Stud Book*, 15.

lambchop whiskers. Whether Oliver Wood spent much time at the local track in Goshen, near Middletown and Unionville, was doubtful. No evidence was found that he raised racehorses on his Minisink farm, so how he came to purchase the weanling roan colt from Daniel VanSickle remains a mystery.

The colt had been foaled in 1858. The youngster likely had no name; the Woods just called him by the familiar name of Dan, or Old Dan, sometime later. His lineage back to Rysdyk's Hambletonian #10 was this: a young man named Lewis Sutton from Warwick acquired a fast mare named Katy Darling, by trade. She had been a lovely, gaited mare but suffered a crippling injury to a front leg. Sutton nursed her back to health and took her to William Rysdyk's two-year-old colt for breeding, hoping to get a fast trotter out of his bargain. Rysdyk's colt—only later to become known as Hambletonian #10—had no name and was not even broken to drive. But that proved no obstacle in the breeding; Katy Darling foaled her colt the following year, in August of 1852.

The colt was born a dark bay with one white hind ankle. He was beautiful, and he would naturally trot alongside his dam in the pasture or on the lead rope. "His reputation began to spread through that horsey region: many men came to see him, and many offers were made and refused for him. At last, when he was seventeen months old, J. S. Edsall and Hezekiah Hoyt drove over from Goshen. They were determined to buy the colt and asked Sutton to price him."[13]

So in the spring of 1854, Sutton sold them the lovely colt for $500, and as Edsall shortly bought out his partner's share, he named the colt Edsall's Hambletonian. The following year, seeking to profit as quickly as possible from his investment, he put the

13 "Alexander's Abdallah and Mr. Redfield," *The Horse Review* 31, no. 17 (April 25, 1905), 442–43.

barely-three-years-old colt into stud service, advertising for the public to bring mares. Edsall also trained the youngster to drive and used him as a road horse, showing his speed at the county fairs.

During his third breeding season, in 1857, Edsall had him bred to seventy-eight mares! One of the many customers brought to Edsall's Hambletonian that season was the unnamed roan mare of Daniel VanSickle.[14] VanSickle had picked her up in New York City from a horse dealer and knew almost nothing of her background. Described as a gal of "fine style and action" with characteristics of a Morgan, she had no pedigree. She foaled in 1858, and when her colt was weaned at about eight months, Oliver Wood bought him from VanSickle.

Since every horseman with aspirations wanted a piece of the Hambletonian name, it was good marketing to name a colt Hambletonian-something during that era. That's where it got confusing, because almost everybody had such an animal. It was a few years later when Oliver Wood began to call his horse Wood's Hambletonian to take advantage of the pedigree and the popularity of his stallion's image. Sometimes in the early years of his career in Deerfield, the horse was also called Hambletonian Jr., but it was not until he acquired his registry number—572—that he was uniquely and permanently named. At home, the stallion was always called Dan. In time, there were so many stallions named Hambletonian that the fledgling breed registry prohibited newly registered stallions to have that name.

---

14 Daniel VanSickle was listed on p. 207 of Vail's Orange County Directory of 1871 as a farmer who owned 230 acres and got his mail at the Goshen post office (HeritageQuest Online).

OLD DAN, UNDATED (COURTESY KNOXVILLE PUBLIC LIBRARY)

REVERSE SIDE OF PHOTOGRAPH WITH HANDWRITTEN LABEL. (COURTESY KNOXVILLE PUBLIC LIBRARY.)

While young Dan was coming to live in the little-known timber section of Pennsylvania—not a prime destination for a rising star on the harness racing scene—it was still a safer place to be than where his sire was headed. In 1859, two Kentucky horsemen went north to Orange County shopping for trotting stallions to enhance the driving stock in that state. They bought from Edsall his young stallion, who at the tender age of seven years had already sired more than two hundred foals in the Hudson Valley region. Most of those offspring had yet to come of trotting age and show their talent on the racetracks.

So it was that the horse who had been known as Edsall's Hambletonian in New York found himself headed to the border state of Kentucky on the eve of the Civil War. Not only did he get a new home, he was going to get a new name as well: Abdallah. His new owners were James Miller and Joel Love, and as time went by the Kentuckians began to call the stallion Love's Abdallah at his digs in Cynthiana, in Harrison County outside Lexington. They charged $25 for a mare to be bred to Love's Abdallah. Even though his owners and a small group of horsemen there wanted better bloodlines in their trotting stock, many Kentucky natives did not share their enthusiasm for a northern stallion. Regional bias was taking a bitter hold during the decade before the war. Love's Abdallah did not breed but a fraction of the number of mares in Kentucky compared to his early life in New York.

After the war broke out, things became even more problematic in the border state. Unmarked troops from both sides raided the fine horse farms of the bluegrass section, stealing horses during the night. As the war dragged on and horses became scarcer, the raids became more frequent. A neighbor of Miller and Love, Robert A. Alexander, owned a quality establishment known as Woodburn

Farm, and he became interested in Love's Abdallah. Alexander was a British citizen, and as the story goes, Miller and Love thought his status as such would make his farm less vulnerable to theft. They sold the stallion to Alexander for $2,500, and after that the horse once again got a new moniker: Alexander's Abdallah.

> The history of Kentucky during the war is so well known as to need but a passing reference. Its geographical position made it one of the "buffer states." Moreover, it at first attempted to preserve a neutral position politically, and the governor refused to furnish the troops demanded by the Federal Government in April, 1861. In August 1861, the state was invaded by the Confederate troops and in November 1861, it gave in its adhesion to the Union. Thereafter the Federal forces held it, almost continuously, until the war closed, but it was not without almost continuous warfare. Large bodies of troops, both Northern and Southern, repeatedly crossed it, many battles and skirmishes were fought, and, in particular, it suffered severely from incessant raids by guerrillas and irregular troops.

> Mr. Alexander had been advised to remove his most valuable horses from the state and did send Pilot, Jr., and others, to Illinois, where he had a brother living. But Abdallah, Bay Chief, and Asteroid, the famous son of [the stallion] Lexington, were among those retained at the farm. On the night of February 2, 1865, Woodburn was raided by Confederate guerrillas and

all three stallions carried off. Federal cavalry stationed near Lexington was despatched [sic] in pursuit and scattered them, next morning, after a skirmish, in which Bay Chief was killed. Asteroid was recovered unharmed, but Abdallah was captured by a soldier who, it is said, refused to give him up to the agents of Mr. Alexander and rode him off. He was unshod and in no condition for hard usage, and after a gallop of 40 or 50 miles he gave out and was turned loose. He was found in a distressing plight next day by men sent from Woodburn, who started home with him, but at Lawrenceburg he was taken with pneumonia and died two or three days later. This was about February 6 or 7, 1865. He had been 12 years old the previous August 22.[15]

Another account of Abdallah's demise was briefly listed by the early compiler of trotting records, John H. Wallace: "Abdallah 15 . . . kept at Woodburn Farm until killed by soldiers, Feb. 2, 1865. Record 2:42."[16] The details of the stallion's death varied, but the end result was the same. The stallion, in the prime years of his life, became a casualty in the bitter, long war just a few weeks from its conclusion. So close and yet so far.

Countless fine horses of the Thoroughbred running type, the trotting type, and the Morgan type were lost on the battlefields. Displaced from their farms, their pedigrees became irrelevant when they were pressed into service by the armies of the Potomac or

---

15 "Alexander's Abdallah," *The Horse Review*, April 25, 1905, 442–43.

16 John Hankins Wallace, *Wallace's Year-Book of Trotting and Pacing in 1890*, Vol. VI, 389, (New York: Wallace Trotting Register Company, 1891), Hathitrust Digital Library.

Northern Virginia. The war stirred up the nation's horse supply, disrupted the breeding programs of many good farms, and brought financial ruin to some southern breeding establishments.

Abdallah's (Alexander's Abdallah #15) offspring from his brief stint in Kentucky, however, became his most important contribution to the Standardbred heritage. Two of his Kentucky colts, later known as Almont #33 and Belmont #64—southern half-brothers to Dan—would rise to the top as studs in the sporting horse world over the coming years. Back up north, Dan was becoming known as Wood's Hambletonian, a sire of fast horses in his own right. He was safe and thriving at his out-of-the-way home in Tioga County.

Meanwhile back in Orange County, New York, where Dan and his sire, Abdallah, had come from, a young mare was still running free in her pasture, untrained. The mare, foaled in 1857, was a daughter of Abdallah and one of those plentiful half-siblings of Dan, Almont, and Belmont. She would be acquired by Wood's former neighbor, Alden Goldsmith. This older sister of Dan would not be broken to drive until she was eight years old. Goldsmith would train the high-strung, wild mare into the fastest record-breaker of the postwar era: Goldsmith Maid.[17]

---

17 At Buffalo Driving Park she trotted a 2:14 mile on August 12, 1872, which held as the new record for several years and made her one of the earliest famous trotters. An illustration of her at this park was published in *Harper's Weekly*, August 12, 1872.

CHAPTER 2

KILBURN JIM: BROOKFIELD TO BIG TIME

Jonas Kilburn was born in 1842 in Orwell, Vermont. His folks, whose name was also spelled in variations Kilbourne and Kilbourn, bought a farm and emigrated to Brookfield Township in Tioga County, Pennsylvania, in 1854. Like many of his peers, he came of age fighting for the Union during the Civil War. He enlisted at age nineteen and spent the next four years with Company F of the Forty-Fifth Regiment of the Pennsylvania Volunteer infantry, seeing action from the Shenandoah to Vicksburg and back. He worked his way up to the rank of sergeant. In the hellish fires and chaos of Virginia's Battle of the Wilderness in May of 1864, he lay injured for three days before being picked up and transported for treatment of his leg wound. Recovered sufficiently to rejoin his regiment, he marched with his comrades in the Grand Review before President Lincoln in Washington, DC, in May of 1865.[18] He was officially mustered out of service in July of 1865.

---

18 W. David Kilburn, 2016.

JONAS KILBURN, AUSTINBURG, PENNSYLVANIA.[19]

---

19 Sexton, *History of Tioga County*, 437.

Exactly when he made his way home was not known, but one thing was certain: he wasted no time in paying Oliver Wood a visit. Having seen some bad times in his young life, Jonas was happy to be alive and grateful to be home. Although he carried painful shrapnel in his knee, he had a little money in his pocket and optimism for his future. His mare was from Canada, and she was bred right away. She foaled her bay colt at the Kilburn farm north of Knoxville in late June 1866. Did Oliver Wood yet realize the potential of his stud? This foal was one of the first offspring of Wood's stallion, and the local farmers and businessmen of the rural region were just beginning to catch the fever for trotting horses that had taken hold of the Hudson Valley and East Coast just prior to the war.

Jonas raised the colt, trained him to drive near home, and took him to see how he measured up against his neighbors on the brand-new track at Academy Corners. The intersection just east of Knoxville was a thriving little crossroads at the time where the small road known as Yarnall Brook, now known as Merrick Hill Road, came down off Butler Hill from the south. It crossed the Cowanesque River and joined the river road leading east or west between Osceola and Westfield. A post office, several stores, a hotel, and a blacksmith shop served as the backdrop to the main establishment, the secondary boarding school known as the Union Academy. There students from the surrounding areas who had completed their required eighth-grade educations could continue for a fee per term. Many lived there in the residence halls that flanked the main building, supervised by a male head teacher and female preceptress.[20]

With the academy drawing its pupils and the crossroads merchants serving the outlying farmers and lumbermen, the little

---

20 Meginness,*Tioga County History*, 418.

junction was a bustling place for local horsemen to meet. At the end of the war in 1865, several local horsemen leased from the farmer Caleb Short a large, flat tract in the field north of the intersection and fitted out an oval racecourse for trotting. The men in this group included Oliver L. Wood's older son, known as O. H. Wood (to distinguish him from his father), Nelson Ray, and Martin V. Purple, both of whom lived nearby.[21] Brothers Will and Joseph Wood were partners in the venture as well. Determined to imitate on a small scale the popular racecourses like the Beacon

JOSEPH WOOD, KNOXVILLE, PENNSYLVANIA.

Course on Long Island and in Goshen, New York, they built a half-mile track with banked corners like the venues popping up all over the northeast to meet the growing appetite for fast road horses. They organized events under the title Knoxville Driving Park Association and called their racetrack the Knoxville Driving Park. O. H. Wood headed up the group as the named president to whom entries for the early race meets were to be given.

They opened the track for business in the summer of 1866 and advertised in the Addison paper for their first annual exhibition of horses to be held at the end of September. They included draft horses and road horses in their judging classes, as well as mares and foals. The admission price was twenty-five cents without a horse or one dollar to enter a horse, with owner's admission included. The

---

21 Sexton, *History of Tioga County*, 235.

**WILLIAM C. WOOD,
KNOXVILLE, PENNSYLVANIA.**

debut event was capped on the third day with a hundred-dollar sweepstakes purse offered for the winner of a trotting race, the first-place horse to get seventy-five dollars and twenty-five dollars to the second-place horse. The residents of Addison, Woodhull, and Troupsburg were invited to enter their animals as well.[22]

In time the association added a row of stables, a small roofed section of bleachers that they ventured to call a grandstand, and an elevated judges' platform with a full view of the whole layout; and they enclosed the area in a solid fence with entrance gates.[23] Replicated later at the Westfield fairgrounds where the Cowanesque Valley High School now stands, at Tioga as described in a subsequent chapter, and in Wellsboro where the cemetery now is located off Nichols Street, it signaled the beginning of the trotting horse era in Tioga County. The driving park became a community hub in the following years, hosting baseball games and encampments of GAR reunions. The nearby hotel was the voting place for township citizens during several elections. In the 1870s, Fourth of July celebrations at the track included fireworks and picnics with footraces.

Jonas's colt was foaled the same summer the Academy Corners track opened for business, and that nearby oval was where he did

---

22 *Addison Advertiser*, September 26, 1866, <u>fultonhistory.com</u>.

23 Ed Wagner, unpublished memorandum and sketched map of Academy Corners, July 20, 1956, Knoxville Public Library.

many training miles as he grew to maturity the next few years. In the spring of 1871, Jonas drove his young bay stallion north over the state line to test him at the larger town of Hornellsville, in Steuben County, New York. By this time the horse had a name: Kilburn Jim.

Hornellsville, now known as Arkport, was part of the community now known as Hornell. Hornellsville was a bustling railroad junction where the Buffalo Division of the Erie railway came from the northwest, joined the railroad west to Erie, Pennsylvania, then proceeded southward to Corning, New York, and points beyond. If they boarded there, folks could catch a train overnight to New York City, Chicago, or Buffalo. With its Erie line maintenance and engine works centered there, Hornellsville was one of the most important rail hubs in the upstate region.

Kilburn Jim's speed attracted the attention of horsemen there and caused something of a bidding war. After various offers, which Jonas refused, he made a deal to sell his five-year-old colt to Hornellsville resident Monroe D. VanScoter. The price: $5,000. Monroe D. VanScoter, (1838–1898) known as M. D. or Roey, was a fellow who dabbled in various enterprises from farming and hotel keeping to working as a Pullman conductor. Later he opened a real estate and loan office in that town around 1890.[24] VanScoter enlisted a Hornellsville friend, William Hale, as a partner to come up with the cash for Kilburn Jim.

---

24 Hon. Harlo Hakes, et al., *Landmarks of Steuben County, New York* (Syracuse, NY: D. Mason, 1896), 437.

M. D. VAN SCOTER,

REAL ESTATE AND LOANS,

ESPECIAL ATTENTION GIVEN FARM LOANS.

No. 156 MAIN STREET,   HORNELLSVILLE, N.

MONROE D. VANSCOTER ADVERTISEMENT, 1895.[25]

Kilburn Jim was not gelded, and Jonas had already bred a handful of mares to him. One of these was the mare Miss Miller, owned by Knoxville resident Fred Miller. Fred Miller ended up with a gray colt from this breeding, a colt he later sold, who was raced, registered, and known as Kilburn Jim Jr. #4768.[26] Jonas may have bred and sold other horses from Jim as well, because Eugene M. Griffin (1846–1920), a farmer who lived north of Westfield on the California Road, bought one. "He was fond of his horses and colts and was very proud of one graceful black carriage horse, Rosalyn, the offspring of a famous trotting horse, sold to him by a neighbor, Mr. Kilbourne."[27] Griffin was a peer to Jonas, having served as a young man in the Civil War, after which he returned home to the hills between Knoxville and Westfield to become a lifelong farmer. A handful of other horses whose owners claimed were offspring of

---

25   Hornellsville City Directory, 1895, p. 108, Hornell Public Library.

26   Kilburn Jim Jr. sired the race mare Kitty Kilburn, (Wallace, *Year-Book*, vol. 6, 454).

27   Geneva E. Pierce, *The Romance of a Changing Life* (Westfield, PA:Valley Dollar Saver, 1970), 96.

Kilburn Jim appeared later in Allegany and Steuben counties; these had nebulous pedigrees and could not be verified.

How much attachment Jonas had to his carefully raised stud colt is lost to time. Jonas had his photograph made seated in a high-wheeled jog cart holding Jim's reins. They stood in front of his parents' Greek Revival farm home on the Austinburg road just a bit north of Knoxville. Did Jonas have the picture made knowing he was parting with his colt, or was it to celebrate one of Jim's early race wins?

That the Kilburn family passed the photograph down through five generations, keeping alive the oral tradition of the horse and the knowledge of the exact location of the picture, attested to the pride Jonas had in raising his fine young stallion.[28] The sale money came at a welcome juncture: Jonas got married just a few weeks later. No matter how much time passed, an influx of cash was always helpful during major life events like buying the farm or getting married. Jonas did not appear in the racetrack local news after that, although he listed six head of horse on his farm's roster a few years later for the 1880 agricultural census.[29]

---

28 W. David Kilburn, 2016.

29 United States Government, 1880 Federal Agricultural Census, Brookfield and Deerfield Townships, www.phmc.state.pa.us.

KILBURN JIM IN FRONT OF THE HOME OF JONAS'S FATHER, PETER KILBURN, ON ROUTE 249 NORTH OF KNOXVILLE, AUSTINBURG ROAD. THE HOUSE IS STILL VISIBLE ON THAT ROAD ALTHOUGH THE EXTERIOR HAS BEEN ALTERED. (COURTESY W. DAVID KILBURN.)

VanScoter and Hale closed the deal on July 12, 1871, and wasted no time testing out their new purchase. On August 8, Kilburn Jim was in Buffalo, New York, at the bigger venue of the Buffalo Driving Park. At the time, trotting was structured in one-mile heats. The winner was required to place first in three out of five heats to take half the purse, the second-place scorer took one quarter of the purse, the third-place finisher got 15 percent, and fourth place received 10 percent; no money was paid below fourth place. If there was a disqualification for any reason, such as a flawed start or a horse breaking gait, additional heats would be trotted. If the judges decided that a heat should be thrown out or there were issues with cheating, heats would also be extended. The heats might be done all at once, but the track officials would often intersperse other classes or events in between to make the most of the weather and keep the crowd's attention and the betting folks' enthusiasm. Sometimes horses got a rest in between heats, but not always, and the drivers had to go with the agenda of the day.

Often there would be an exhibition in which a popular or superstar horse would trot or pace against "time"—the clock—with a running horse to stimulate it. Other times there might be a special team exhibition race or even a "wild Indian show" to keep up the excitement for the crowds. If the weather turned stormy, delays could stretch the event into darkness or postpone the completion of the heats to the next day. Harness racing was rife with bribery and race-fixing schemes, and track officials would frequently substitute or switch drivers at the last moment to dispel accusations of cheating.

This was Kilburn Jim's first time out in a big city, and likely his first time shipped on a train. Many new sights and sounds awaited him. His new owners put him in a large class of ten horses. He was distanced, lagging so far behind the pack that his time did not count.

There was much to learn. Kilburn Jim was not in Academy Corners anymore. Two days later, he was started in a class for horses who had never yet achieved a 2:30 mile. Again there was a large field of ten horses, all vying for a piece of the $3,000 purse. There were at least fifteen thousand people in the stands that day, and the betting pools were estimated, or perhaps exaggerated by the track columnist, at more than $200,000.[30]

In *The Kentucky Harness Horse*, Ken McCarr describes betting at harness races during this time: "This form of betting has now vanished but it was the most popular in those days. Each horse in a race would be "auctioned" to the highest bidder and the high bidder on the winning horse would receive all the money in the pool . . . Drivers and owners often bid on their own horse, and when they won the pool might be more than the purse in the race. Because racing in those days was always two or more heats, pools were sold for the entire race, not just individual heats."[31]

This field ran three heats: a horse named Uncle Abe won them all, in 2:37, 2:30 1/4, and 2:27 3/4. While Kilburn Jim placed out of the money and sixth overall, he was catching on. He had stayed with the pack and finished midway down, not at the bottom like two days before. He was learning how to trot in the big time. The race meets at Buffalo would shortly become part of the new Grand Circuit of harness racing, the top level of competition that was still evolving. But the sport had not yet hit its stride, and neither had Kilburn Jim.

"The oldest and biggest of these circuits was formed in 1871 . . . and is known as the Grand Circuit. Originally formed to draw the best horses from the metropolitan areas, a group of tracks in the hinterlands offered good purses so that the rest of the nation could

---

30 "Buffalo Races," *Oswego Daily Palladium*, August 11, 1871, <u>fultonhistory.com</u>.
31 McCarr, 119.

see the best of the horses. Using express trains, the horses went from track to track. Sometimes there were fourteen or more carloads of horses."[32]

In *The Trotting and the Pacing Horse in America*, Hamilton Busbey offers another perspective of the evolving racing circuits expands on the structure: "In 1873 the Quadrilateral Trotting Combination was formed - Cleveland . . . Buffalo . . . Utica . . . and Springfield. The premiums for these four meetings amounted to $169,300, and enthusiasm increased as the horses swept down the line. In 1874 Charter Oak Park at Hartford was opened, and in 1875 there was a clash between the new tracks at Rochester and Poughkeepsie. The Grand Trotting Circuit was thus extended . . ."[33]

Kilburn Jim came back closer to home a few weeks later on August 29 at Addison Driving Park for a small-town purse of $100 for horses who had never gone faster than a 3:00 mile. If a horse had been clocked at a certain time at a sanctioned meet, he could not be entered in a slower class after that time. A horse had to stay at that time and speed level or get better; the owner could not enter the animal against known slower horses just because he was assured his horse could win the purse. Against four other horses, Kilburn Jim won three heats out of five to take first money. The heats were trotted in 2:44, 2:59 1/2, 3:01, 2:57 1/2, and 3:05, and Jim had placed first in the first, second, and fifth heats.

The following day Kilburn Jim went up against a bay gelding who was to become a prime peer and competitor: Ashland Pet, owned by A. Jones from Avon, New York. Together with a feisty bay mare named Young Thorn, who had trotted on the heels of Kilburn Jim in the previous day's race, this threesome came together in a class for

---

32 McCarr, 125.
33 Published by Macmillan Company (1904), 292–93. https://books.google.com.

a purse of $175. Their battle went to six hotly contested heats, which were not finished until after dusk. Young Thorn won the first heat, Jim won the second and third, but Ashland Pet took the fourth and fifth. No one was giving in, and the end, "the sixth one, which was trotted after sundown, Ashland Pet and Kilburn Jim trotting head to head for at least twenty rods,"[34] was a nail-biter. But Ashland Pet won it. How much excitement could there be in Addison?

Kilburn Jim's local fans throughout the region were on hand rooting for him: "Thus on a visit to the Grand Circuit or state fair, people often saw the latest, fastest models of what they had in their home stables—and they tended to form rooting interest based on horses who might be related by blood, albeit distantly, to their own. It was, in other words, a lot like NASCAR, though the enthusiasts were much better dressed."[35] In Kilburn Jim's new home at Hornellsville, the racetrack excitement ran high that summer.

On September 29, Kilburn Jim came up against Ashland Pet again, this time in Cuba, New York. The track at Cuba was an irregularly shaped trapezoidal mile squeezed in the flat land between the stream known as Oil Creek and the Genessee Valley Canal, which had been an important shipping route before rail lines. This day a horse named Cattaraugus Chief would top them both in a five-heat race in which Jim took the first and second heats to come in second money. Kilburn Jim had dropped seconds off his mile heats, with his best ones that day being 2:35 and 2:35 1/2. His race season had wrapped up. He was on break a few months over the winter, and his new owner had high hopes for the next summer season. Van Scoter bought out his partner, Hale, so as to have full control of the horse's

---

34 *Spirit of the Times*, August 30, 1871, <u>fultonhistory.com</u>.
35 Charles Leerhsen, *Crazy Good: The True Story of Dan Patch, the Most Famous Horse in America* (New York: Simon & Schuster, 2008), 11.

training and schedule. Since the 2:35-and-over times for these mile heats were several seconds slower than every horseman's goal of the 2:30 mile, Kilburn Jim had yet to find his niche and train into his optimum speed.

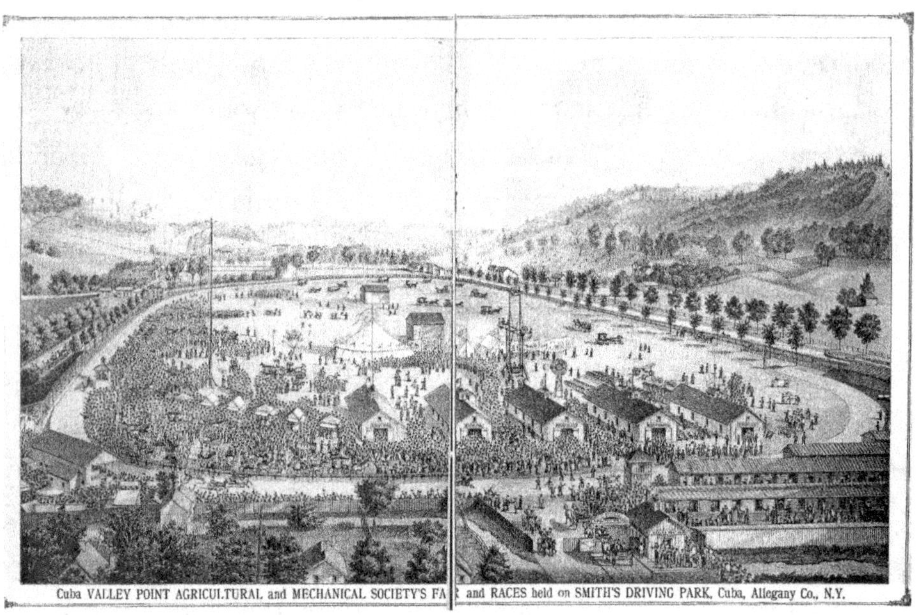

CUBA VALLEY POINT AGRICULTURAL SOCIETY'S FAIR AND RACES HELD ON SMITH'S DRIVING PARK, CUBA, ALLEGANY COUNTY, NEW YORK.[36]

After a winter's rest, the winter snows melted and the dirt roads dried out, Kilburn Jim put some spring training miles under his harness. Jim was fresh to start near home in Addison, New York, on June 13, 1872. He won all three heats over two other competitors, Barney and Lady Barber, to win the class in 2:45, 2:45, and 2:43. The following weekend found him back at home in Hornellsville on June 20 for a $250 purse, in which he again won all three heats in faster

---

36 *Atlas of Allegany County, New York* (New York: D. G. Beers & Co., 1869).

times: 2:42, 2:37, and 2:36. Things were looking sweet for the summer. The very next day, he took on Ashland Pet again with two others to win all three heats of this race in 2:36 1/2, 2:36 1/2, and 2:36. His miles of training were starting to pay off as he dropped seconds off his times.[37]

July was quiet on Jim's calendar, except for a trip back to Academy Corners on July 24. At his old stomping grounds, VanScoter entered him in the 2:35 trotting class, which he won in three heats. Jim had moved up in the world, and he was able to show his old friends and home fans that he was quite a bit faster than when he had been at Knoxville before. Were the Woods on hand that day to watch the youngster bred from their place? There were other trotting classes on tap for the two-day event, and a class for "running horses" in which the horses were ridden as in the Kentucky Derby Thoroughbred style. The Corning paper said there was a "large number of people in town" to attend the meet, and a cornet band from Elmira provided music for the affair.[38]

In midsummer there was news: there would be an upcoming match race that would put Kilburn Jim up against Ashland Pet once more. Match races were one-against-one speed contests with conditions and payouts prearranged by the horses' owners with the track officials. They were publicity events that provided hype for the host track and fodder for boasting, betting, and speculation on the part of owners, fans, trainers, and gamblers. These special races were often put into the middle of the day's race schedule to provide variety and keep race fans in the park. The match was to take place at Buffalo at the beginning of that city's race meeting week, on August 1.

---

37   *Hornellsville Weekly Tribune*, June 21, 1872, <u>fultonhistory.com</u>.
38   *Corning Journal*, July 25, 1872, <u>fultonhistory.com</u>.

The July 8, 1872, *Buffalo Courier & Republic* announced with anticipation that "a match for $1,000 a side, a bona fide affair we are assured, has been made between Ashland Pet and J. H. Kilburn (formerly Kilburn Jim), and will be trotted over the Buffalo Park, August 1st. As the great races draw near, many flyers find their way to Buffalo, and we may anticipate that we shall have abundance of sport to whet our appetites for the carnival of race-week."[39]

When the day came, Kilburn Jim beat his rival from the previous year in three straight heats: 2:30 3/4, 2:33, and 2:32. Each owner took home his $1,000 payout. Each horse had just trotted his new personal best. But neither had yet made their owner's goal, the sought-after mile in 2:30 or less that would put the animal in the new sport's permanent record books.

Jim was stabled at the Buffalo Driving Park for the duration of the week to prepare for the main meeting. On Wednesday, August 7, there were about ten thousand race fans filling the park by the time the sky cleared off for the afternoon's races. Around two o'clock, the officials resumed unfinished heats from the previous day's program. Jim was entered in the third race of the day, the 2:34 class, which boasted a $5,000 purse. Six horses were slated to run; one was withdrawn before it started. There had been ahead of time much gossip and speculation about the merits of an unknown challenger. Buffalo resident J. L. Doty had just purchased a bay gelding called Jim Irving from Kentucky. The newcomer took the first heat, but in the second heat Kilburn Jim got ahead by several lengths when Jim Irving broke gait but then overtook Kilburn Jim with a surge so astounding that the racegoers and officials suspected Kilburn Jim's driver had been bribed to hold him back:

---

39 This is only reference to the proposed name change found. Nowhere else does the horse appear by that name.

"He closed rapidly on Kilburn Jim, who was leading the field . . . and passed the latter, coming in two lengths ahead. Considerable feeling was manifested at the result, and the driver of Kilburn Jim was accused of having held him in. The judges, after consultation, changed drivers, placing Kilburn Jim under Dan Mace's guidance. The last heat, however, dispelled all doubts, Irving winning the heat and the race by several lengths."[40]

Kilburn Jim finished second money behind the new guy in town, and his gambling backers and fans were not pleased.

There was no rest for him. The next day dawned hotter at the Buffalo Park, but Kilburn Jim was on tap again, this day entered in the 2:30 class for a lucrative $10,000 purse. Van Scoter's horse had gained a following, the bettors knew his name, and he was not stopping now. The daily paper happily reported that the stands were full of enthusiastic fans, most of them betting, and the breeze was pleasant so as to keep folks cool on a hot August day. Though it may be hard to fully take in what an average day at the races entailed back then, it was a comfort to know that "the crowd was in good humor . . . We heard of no arrests and no cases of pocket picking."[41]

The day's favorite was a mare named Gazelle, with the bettors' second pick being a gal named Lucille Golddust; Kilburn Jim was ranked third in the betting before the first heat. There were seven other horses vying for a piece of the $10,000 pie. Jim Irving was not in this mix. Dan Mace was again driving Jim, and they started off in the center of the field. By the first quarter pole, Mace had taken Jim to the lead by a length. By the last half, Jim opened the gap to four lengths and stayed ahead of everyone to win the heat in 2:25. All eyes and opera glasses in the grandstands were now on Jim as the

---

40 *New York Herald*, August 8, 1872, 5, <u>fultonhistory.com</u>.
41 *Buffalo Courier & Republic*, August 9, 1872, <u>fultonhistory.com</u>.

second heat began, and he led off, getting a six-length lead on the next-closest rival. Gazelle made a move to catch him and closed the gap by a few lengths the last half of the heat but could not get to Jim, and he came away three lengths ahead of her and everyone else to take that heat as well. That heat was Jim's new best: 2:23!

The *Buffalo Courier & Republic* reported it thus:

> THIRD HEAT—This was a glorious heat. The betting was about three to one on Kilburn Jim against the field. They got away on the fourth trial, Kilburn Jim and Gazelle having an even start, and such a race as they made of it was beautiful to see. The stallion went the fastest and as they spun around the first turn Gazelle had her nose at his wheel, she held it just there, and the quarter-pole was passed, in 25, with one length separating the horses. As they flew up the back stretch, at a 2.15 gait, every eye was fastened on the struggle. The mare gradually drew up, and every inch she gained was noted by ten thousand spectators. Half way to the half-mile pole she collared the stallion and for a few strides they went like a double team, but those who sympathized with Gazelle were sorry to see her give back a little, and when Kilburn Jim passed the half, in 1.00, he was half a length ahead.[42]

Two lengths behind and lagging, Gazelle fell back, and the rest of the horses behind her shifted positions as they all grew tired. Even Jim slacked off ever so slightly as his rivals fell away, and he won that

---

42 Ibid.

heat as well to take first-place money, a slower heat of 2:25 1/4. It had been a big day for Kilburn Jim, and for VanScoter. Kilburn Jim's 2:23 time was to stand as his best record and assured his spot in the Standardbred archives, and VanScoter got his $5,000 investment recouped in one payoff. The gambling folks were happy, too, because even though Jim's odds went down as his image rose, they had made out well for the first heats: "His backers picked up a great deal of money, and most of it was won at long odds."[43]

Were the Wood Brothers following their Academy Corners track friend in the papers? The brand new Grand Circuit, or Quadrilateral Trotting Combination, as the new network of race meets was calling itself, was rolling along through the late summer, and Utica, New York, was next on the schedule. Once again, Kilburn Jim got aboard the train.

Utica Park was brand new, so new that the streets leading to it were not finished when the throngs arrived for the race meet. The glowing news accounts indicated that the sections of the grandstand reserved for ladies who came for the races unescorted were of the best caliber, and that it should become a desirable venue for the demurest of ladies to enjoy racing. Utica Park also afforded plentiful betting pool offices where folks could buy a ticket on a horse in between heats as his popularity rose or fell.

The Kentucky gelding Jim Irving's victory recently earned in his new hometown of Buffalo loomed large in peoples' minds, and he was the New York gamblers' heavy favorite as the pools were sold for the first of the heats in the 2:34 race on Wednesday, August 14. Rounding out the field for the $3,000 purse in this class were the stallions Joe Brown, William Turnbull, and Kilburn Jim, one gelding,

---

43 Ibid.

Ben Flagler, and a mare named Jennie (also spelled Jenny and owned by a fellow named Abram Johnson, to distinguish her from dozens of other Standardbred trotting mares in the record books named Jenny). When Kilburn Jim led the pack for the entire heat to win it in 2:29 1/4, the jubilant ones were mostly from the rural counties of the state.

There must have been at least some of Jim's local following on hand to collect money, because the *Utica Daily Observer* columnist had this to say about the upset of the evening: "A number of green country lads from Utica, Lowville, Clinton, Herkimer, Deerfield . . . and other places saw the New Yorkers for quite at large sum last evening . . . There were more greenies about the pool offices getting their cards cashed than there were New Yorkers."[44] "New Yorkers" referred to those from downstate, New York City, but who was there, in fact, betting from Deerfield?

The remainder of the race would be finished Thursday, and just after two o'clock they got the second heat underway. Kilburn Jim started near the back of the field, and it was very close, with all the horses "lapped upon each other in order," according to the *Utica Daily Observer*.[45] The article continues:

> Irving shot ahead in the second quarter, leading Joe Brown at the half-mile post by half a length in 1:13 1/2, Turnbull third, Flagler fourth, Kilburn Jim fifth and Jennie sixth. At the third quarter pole Irving led, with Brown, Flagler, Turnbull, Kilburn Jim and Jennie following. On the home stretch the flyers came in in splendid shape, Irving leading and taking the

---

44 *Utica Daily Observer*, August 16, 1872, <u>fultonhistory.com</u>.

45 Ibid.

heat in 2:23 1/2, followed closely by Joe Brown and Jennie, who acted beautifully on the home stretch, and Kilburn Jim and Flagler following close behind . . . When the time was announced there was great cheering, and then every New York man put up his pile on Irving . . .

At 3:30 P.M. the horses were sent off for the third heat of the 2:34 race. Kilburn Jim led, Turnbull, Flagler, Joe Brown, Irving and Jennie following in order. At the turn Kilburn was ahead, with Irving close on to him, Flagler, Brown, Jennie and Turnbull in the rear. Kilburn Jim was at the quarter pole in 35, Irving, Flagler, Brown and Turnbull moving in the order named. At the half pole Kilburn Jim flew by in 1:09 3/4, Irving knitting up closely, Flagler, Turnbull, Joe Brown and Jennie doing their level best. At the three-quarter pole Kilburn Jim and Irving were head and head, and then every man, woman and child stood up and all seemed to cheer at one time. Flagler and Turnbull followed the first pair. Down the home-stretch Irving gained on Kilburn Jim, gaining the heat in 2:24 1/4, Flagler, Brown, Turnbull and Jennie in order.

There was almost another hour and a half before the fourth heat was called, and in that time good old Dan Mace was put in as Jennie's driver. Had there been dissatisfaction with her performance or something fishy going on? The other excitement in the stands attracting attention was that "a country man fell into the hands of the police." Too much celebrating with the flask? Wonder who he was rooting for...

It was around five o'clock when the fourth heat got underway:

Jennie got off first, with Kilburn Jim second, Irving third, Turnbull fourth, Flagler fifth and Joe Brown so close to Flagler that the sulkies collided, without causing any particular injury to them. Irving passed to the front on the turn, leaving Kilburn Jim and Jennie behind. At the quarter, Irving and Kilburn Jim were lapped, making it in 35 seconds, Kilburn Jim breaking a little, Jennie, Turnbull, Joe Brown and Flagler bringing up the rear. At the half-mile post, wonderful to relate, Irving fell to the rear of all, Kilburn Jim making it first in 1:11 3/4, followed by Jennie, Turnbull, Flagler, Joe Brown and Irving. Then the New Yorkers' spirits drooped. At the three-quarter pole Kilburn Jim led, Jennie, Turnbull, Flagler, Joe Brown and Irving following all in a bunch. Down the home stretch they flew, Kilburn Jim still ahead. Irving made a terrific burst of speed and gained for an instant, but broke inside of the stretch. Jennie and Flagler did their level best and came down together, each one trying to get alongside of Kilburn Jim, but they couldn't do it. Brown and Turnbull were abreast in the rear, and then the crowd yelled and cheered vociferously. The heat was won by Kilburn Jim in 2:27

1/2, and he was followed in order by Jennie, Flagler, Joe Brown, Turnbull and Irving.[46]

Everyone was in a lather by this time. A near-crash at the start, an unsuccessful rush to overtake the leader, the spectators shouting on their feet, the favorite trailing at the end: adrenaline seeped through the musty newsprint—digitized and shrunken almost beyond legibility—more than 140 years later!

At 6:00 p.m. they started the fifth heat. Kilburn Jim led off, and though several of the others came for him . . .

> . . . he kept his place in the lead, passing the pole in 1:12, Irving second, Jennie and the others following. At the three-quarter pole Kilburn Jim led Irving about a head, with Jennie close in the rear. Irving broke badly in the home stretch, and Jennie and Brown went by him. Kilburn Jim rushed toward the judges' stand under the whip in 2:28, with Jennie, Brown, Irving, Turnbull and Flagler following in order. The heat was finished at 6:15 P.M. There was great excitement for a few moments over the result. One of Kilburn Jim's friends embraced his driver affectionately, proving his regard for him by biting his ear. That fellow undoubtedly held a $100 pool card which he had bought for $15.[47]

Kilburn Jim took first money that night; it was Jim Irving's turn to take second. With the perspective that time and record books

---

46 Ibid.
47 Ibid.

provide, it seems clear they were truly peers: they shared the same trotting record, what would now be called a "personal best": 2:23. Kilburn Jim's had been made the hot August 8 just the week previous to their Utica standoff. Jim Irving would get his own record but not until three years later, in Springfield, Massachusetts, on August 25, 1875. There was always someone to be knocked out of the winner's circle.

Rain set in that evening, and all the next day's races were postponed. Jim Irving's entourage departed Utica in the wake of his defeat, but VanScoter kept Kilburn Jim there for another run. The 2:30 class was on tap next, where Jim would face off against Jennie again with others for a plush $6,000 purse. They got an unexpected rest in their stables due to the pouring rain all day Thursday, and it was Saturday afternoon, August 17, when the horses finally got back out on the track to warm up for the day's events.

Jim started strong and won the first two heats boldly in 2:26 and 2:26 1/2, but he couldn't hold off Jennie this time: she showed bursts of speed that overtook Jim and the others to win the last three heats and take first money. Jim had to settle for second money this time, earning $1,500 cash for VanScoter to round out their big week in Utica.[48]

VanScoter loaded Kilburn Jim on the railway, and they headed back west across the state to the town of Medina, in Orleans county. On August 29, Kilburn Jim beat one other contender there, Gray Mack, in three heats to win first money, half of a $400 purse.

VanScoter's hometown paper, the *Hornellsville Daily Standard*, proudly published that same week: "Kilburn Jim is now six years old. His best record is 2:23, at Utica. [Dan] Mace, who has driven him

---

48 Walter T. Chester, *Chester's Complete Record of Trotting and Pacing From the Earliest Dates to the Close of 1883* (Chicago: Walter T. Chester, 1884).

lately, pronounces him the honestest trotter he ever drew rein over. Taking into consideration his age, and the amount of training he has had, many good judges believe that he will make, if no bad luck befalls him, the fastest trotter in the world. In the last seventeen days he has earned for his owner $10,500 in purses won."[49]

From there, VanScoter and Mace took Jim west to Cleveland, Ohio, by September 13 for a larger purse of $1,200 as part of the Fall Trotting Circuit at the larger track there. Once again, Jim took all three heats over four rivals in his class to win that race. His times were clinging right around the 2:30 mark, deviating only within one second each heat.[50]

Grand Rapids, Michigan, was the next stop on the stallion's Midwestern itinerary, and he made it there before September 20. Whom should he meet there but his earlier competitor, Jennie, who was also in fine form. They met up in the same class with three other horses, all going for a piece of the $1,200 purse in that city. Jennie finally won the race, but Kilburn Jim made her work for it, taking the second and fourth heats himself to win second place and extending it into six heats. Jim got no rest in Grand Rapids; he trotted the very next day, losing to a gelding named Red Cloud. In a field of seven with the fastest heat trotted in 2:28, Jim managed to get second money.[51]

Jim had to deal with Jennie one more time, in Indianapolis, Indiana, on October 2. In a field of seven in the 2:25 class with a $3,500 purse, he faltered, ending up out of the money. Two days later on October 4, he started in a field of six for a purse of $500 but was distanced and out of the race after the third heat; he did not finish.

---

49 *Hornellsville Daily Standard*, August 29, 1872, <u>fultonhistory.com</u>.
50 Chester, *Complete Record*.
51 Ibid.

One has to wonder whether VanScoter ever doubted Kilburn Jim's stamina during this time. Kilburn Jim came east after Indianapolis, stopping back in Utica for a race on October 17. There Jim won once more, showing his consistency in three straight heats of 2:32 1/2, 2:35, and 2:32, over a mare named Kitty Gavin and a rival he had lost to in Cuba the previous summer, the bay gelding named Cattaraugus Chief. The purse was $500; as first place Kilburn Jim took home half.

VanScoter then took Jim home, having traveled hundreds of miles by rail that summer. Jim had started in eighteen races and had earned $18,500 that busy season. VanScoter expected even better things to come in the summer of 1873.

But it was not to be; Kilburn Jim took sick and got worse. On November 29, the young stallion died at home in his barn. At age six, Jim would barely have had his adult molars to be considered a mature horse. VanScoter stated that the horse had contracted flatulent colic and inflammation of the bowels; other sources claimed the ailment was, in fact, lung fever, now known as pneumonia. Whichever the case, the beloved bay had been sick about ten days. VanScoter was shocked and disappointed, natural for a small-time horseman in such a situation. He had made the big circuit with his flashy stallion, and his local friends were saddened as well. He claimed he had turned down a $20,000 offer on the horse a few weeks before, thinking his value should rise the following summer.

Kilburn Jim's demise was chronicled more than most. He was a four-legged celebrity, at least in his upstate region and across the border into Tioga County. His death notice appeared in several New York state papers: the *Albany Evening Times*, the *New York Sun*, the *Canandaigua Ontario Repository & Messenger*, and more. Together with sadness for his owner, the details of VanScoter's financial loss were repeated in each account, almost with relish. Many an amateur horseman operating his cash flow close to his vest pocket might have read the news of VanScoter's misfortune and squirmed. How many small-town horsemen playing in the sport at the tracks were just one dead horse from financial ruin?

Kilburn Jim's original owner, Jonas Kilburn, got his money and stayed with his farm. Although he had shrapnel in his knee from the war that pained him the remainder of his days, he made a living, built a house of his own, raised a family, and had a farm to pass down to his son when he died in 1902.

VanScoter was not, however, easily discouraged. He moved from Hornellsville south to Pennsylvania in 1876, and took ownership of the Academy Corners hotel, called the Cowanesque House, next to the driving park there. He now lived in the neighborhood of the three Wood brothers. He would continue to dabble in horses over the next few years, and he would put Wood horses on the Grand Circuit again. O. H. Wood had a sharp roan mare, named Blue Mare, also a daughter of Old Dan. Drawn to the harness tracks like a moth to the flame, the optimistic and tenacious VanScoter bought her and put her on the Grand Circuit during the seasons of 1877 and 1878, as a peer to her famous half sister, Nancy Hackett.

Kilburn Jim was the earliest of the offspring of Wood's Hambletonian to get into the lucrative races in upstate New York that became part of the Grand Circuit. He was the first of the trotting family from Knoxville to qualify for entry into the fledgling National Trotting Association Standardbred register books. In so doing he ushered his sire into the registry as well: their stallion numbers are recorded in order as Kilburn Jim #571 and next his sire, Wood's Hambletonian #572. According to the association rules in effect at that time, a horse was eligible to be entered into the

Standardbred registry if it had trotted or paced a mile in 2:30 or less in an officially sanctioned race or if it had sired an animal that had achieved that mile time. With his 2:23 mile on August 8, 1872, at Buffalo, Kilburn Jim paved the way for more siblings and a score of Wood horse descendants to arrive on the racing scene. There were foals born that year in Tioga County who would do exactly that.

CHAPTER 3

NANCY HACKETT: ADVERTISING EXPENSE

Nancy Hackett was in the second wave of Old Dan's offspring to win on the Grand Circuit, and in so doing she raised his reputation as a sire of fast stock. She was a roan, taking her coloring from her sire. Her dam, unknown by any other name than Hackett Mare in the records, was owned by a farmer of modest means named Elmer Hackett (1823–1901). His farm was up the Broughton Hollow road out of Westfield, Pennsylvania, and like everyone in those days he had a team of two horses, but his farm was small and his primary livestock was a flock of sheep.

Oral tradition has it that Hackett brought the mare with a "drove" of horses from Vermont, but the date of that journey is not known. *Wallace's Year Book* listed Nancy Hackett's breeder as "E. Hackett, Westfield, PA,"[52] not the Woods, so they perhaps did not own the Hackett Mare at first but acquired her sometime later. The date of Nancy Hackett's foaling is also not certain; she was likely born in 1870. The Hackett Mare was bred to Old Dan several different years, producing the brown gelding Argonaut about two years after Nancy, a road mare named Celia Taylor, who was not raced,

____

52 John Hankins Wallace, *Wallace's Year-Book of Trotting and Pacing*, vol. 6, 519.

and another mare named Maud Hackett, who was a broodmare at the Babcock Farm near Hornellsville by 1892.[53]

Nancy Hackett was one of the few horses for whom a primary source had been kept by the Wood family. It was a stereopticon card with the handwritten inscription "Nancy Hacket Wood" on the back. It bore the printed logo of "T. E. Wood, Photographic Artist, Goshen, N.Y." The card surfaced among the items of Earle Robbins, husband of Edna Wood Robbins, daughter of Joseph Wood.

VERSO INSCRIPTION "NANCY HACKET WOOD" ON THOMAS E. WOOD PHOTO STOCK. UNIDENTIFIED, UNDATED. (COURTESY BARBARA ROBBINS COBB.)

---

53 *Hornellsville Weekly Tribune*, March 30, 1894, <u>fultonhistory.com</u>.

That the card bore Thomas E. Wood's imprint and remained among the few artifacts in the family's possession indicated that Nancy Hackett was a favorite whom someone in the family had followed to the big time. Was she one of the horses the Woods attempted to race themselves? Many of the offspring of Old Dan were sold by their breeders and changed hands several times during their careers on the plentiful, small-town tracks of the northeast. Did Joseph Wood sit by the stove in the evenings reading *Spirit of the Times* or *Wallace's Monthly* to keep up with what his stud's offspring were achieving for others?

How the Woods acquired Nancy was a mystery. Most of the offspring of Old Dan were foaled at the farm of the breeder, the owner of the mare. As long as the stud fee was fully paid, the foal was born the property of the mare's owner. It seemed that at some point the Hackett Mare was acquired by Woods. It then followed that Woods were repeatedly breeding her to Old Dan and had the offspring to sell to others. It seemed unlikely that Elmer Hackett returned each year for the stud's services and sold the colts himself. There was little evidence that Hackett was breeding other horses or was a racing enthusiast. His entries in the agricultural census for the years 1850 and 1880 revealed the inventory of a farmer who subsisted on a small acreage of rocky, hilly terrain. There was for Hackett no margin of cash with which to dabble in sporting horses.

Nancy was trained and tested initially at the Academy Corners driving park near home, and was entered by Will and Joseph Wood as "Wood Bros." in her early races. She made her public debut in Oswego, New York, at the beginning of July, 1875, where she trotted seven heats against seven other horses. She won the second and third heats in 2:46 and placed in the money.

In the fall of 1876, Nancy Hackett trotted trials at the Berry's Driving Park nearer home in Tioga, Pennsylvania. This racecourse was a one-mile track between the creek and the main road, on a flat field now occupied by Tyoga Container and the building formerly known as Treat's Hardware. It was built by Thomas J. Berry (1841–1879), whose farm buildings sat across the road now known as Route 287. The remains of outbuildings are still visible, as is a portion of the once-elegant Greek-columned residence, hinting at the prosperity projected by Berry during the trotting era. On September 13, Nancy made a respectable showing in a field of four, placing in the money by taking the second and fifth heats in a contest that went to six heats and stretched into the next day. The winner was a Tioga mare, Lou Gibbs, owned by local W. M. Gibbs. Nancy's best times in that race were an unremarkable 2:46 mile, nothing to indicate her potential.[54]

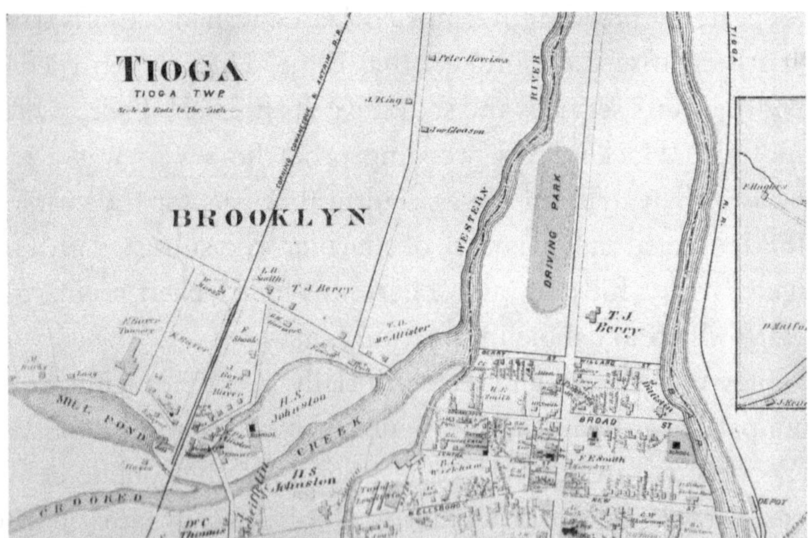

VILLAGE OF TIOGA IN 1875, ATLAS OF TIOGA COUNTY, PENNSYLVANIA, F.W. BEERS & CO., NEW YORK, 1875 P.52

---

54 *Chester, Trotting and Pacing Record,* 461.

A few weeks later at the end of September, the Woods took Nancy to Elmira, New York. That race was likely at the Eldridge Park track on the west side of the city, as the track at Maple Avenue was built later in the 1880s. She went against three others but could not lower her time, and all three heats were taken by an Elmira gelding who was going about three seconds faster than Nancy had yet been able to achieve.

The following year, the Wood brothers kept her in training during the summer and entered her only in the Fall Trotting Circuit in the Midwest. They put her on the railway to Columbus, Ohio, for the meet on October 9, 1877. She was up against a large field in a faster class, and she dropped almost ten seconds off her previous year's time. She took one heat out of five total in 2:30, which put her in third money. Joseph and Will Wood must have felt her training was going to pay off, for they were dabbling in the racing circuits much farther from their home farm back in Tioga County. Was either of them traveling with Nancy, or had they entrusted her to someone else? If one of them was traveling with her, the fall was a logical time for them because the farmer's harvest would have been winding down by October, allowing one of them to take her out.

Nancy boarded the train directly from there and headed southwest to Cincinnati, Ohio, where she trotted on October 16, scoring again in the money by winning one heat in 2:30, a faster time than she had yet attained. The purse was $1,000 this time, and she had six rivals, so she likely won third money that day. There was no rest for her; she arrived in Indianapolis, Indiana, for the October 23 meet, where she trotted in a field of six but won no heats in her race. Learning the life of a trotter on the circuit, she rode the train for hundreds of miles, then settled into a new stall every week in a different city. She stayed in Indianapolis, and three days later she won one heat out of four in a contest with two competitors. They were all a bit slow that day, and Nancy's time was 2:40 1/2, but it earned her second money of a $500 purse.[55]

Not yet ready to bring her home, the Woods shipped Nancy down to Madison, Indiana, and got her there for the first of November. In Madison, she slugged it out with four other horses that were so well-matched the race went to eight tough heats. Nancy won two heats out of eight, and likely earned second money in that 2:40 class.[56] Nancy was trotting a 2:38 1/2. That circuit had drawn to a close, and she came home for a rest over the winter.

The Woods had seen on Nancy's sojourn through the trotting circuit of the Midwest that they had a fast, tough, and competitive mare on their hands. Nancy had learned to ride the rails and thread her way through a pack of rivals around the track. She might be speckled and a bit small, but she could hold her own.

After a winter's rest at home and regular workouts, she shaved seconds off her times, and in the spring of 1878, the Wood fellows had high expectations for Nancy. They entered her in all five meets of the Grand Circuit, from Cleveland, Ohio, to Hartford, Connecticut—the big time—in the lucrative and noteworthy 2:26 classes. Before the beginning of July, she was taken to Rochester, New York, and put in the charge of trainer John Hounstein. This elusive guy (track writers spelled his name no less than six different ways) made his living at the track. Hounstein was listed in the 1882 edition of the *Turfmen's Directory* as a trainer and driver who lived at the Rochester Driving Park. At least that was where he got his mail

---

55 Ibid., 164, 441.
56 Ibid., 598.

in the winter months. During the summer racing season he trundled all over the country riding the railcars with horses.[57]

He began Nancy's daily workouts in earnest at that venue under the scrutiny of friends and competitors.[58] Railbirds called her a "little roan" and sportswriters watched the action each morning and fed the trotting gossip to the public in the newspapers. Nancy was, as we would now say, *hot*, and her workouts were chronicled in the daily papers and horse journals with excitement and expectation. "A horse who could pace a mile in 2:30 in those days could be competitive at the smaller fairs, and every second below that was significant in terms of the class you raced in, and the purse money you could win. A 2:20 horse, for example, could bring a man considerable local prestige, and pick up four or five hundred bucks in the bargain."[59]

Hounstein was training other horses as well and had along with him a full brother to Nancy, the brown gelding Argonaut, whom the track watchers and columnists also loved. Argonaut was six years old at the time. Hopes were high as Nancy kicked things off on the Grand Circuit for the summer season of 1878 in Cleveland, Ohio, in the fast, pricey 2:26 class, where the purses ranged around $1,500. On July 27, she slugged it out with eight other horses, some of whom, like Lady Voorhees, Bonesetter, and Wolford Z., she would meet again soon on the Grand Circuit. The race went a full five heats and was won by the grey gelding Steve Maxwell. Nancy did not place in the money that day, but she proved she could play in the game. She was no longer a big horse at a little track; she was a little mare in the big time.

---

57   *Turfmen's Directory*, 1882, Hathitrust Digital Library.
58   *Spirit of the Times*, July 15, 1878.
59   Leerhsen, *Crazy Good*, 71.

Nancy Hackett's big day came just one week later on August 3, 1878, at the Buffalo meeting. More than ten thousand people were in attendance, and the day was warm and sunny with a light breeze. In a field of eight horses, she trotted five heats, placing first in three of them to win the 2:26 class. Even though she started off at the bottom for the first two heats, her rivals like Lady Voorhees, Bonesetter, and Wolford Z. could not hold her off, and John Murphy's gray gelding, Steve Maxwell, who had topped the class in Cleveland, ended well below Nancy.

Of the fourth heat, as Bonesetter and Wolford Z. battled it out with Nancy, the *Spirit of the Times* wrote: "It was a magnificent struggle home between these three, every inch of ground being hotly contested; but her followers could not gain a foot on Nancy Hackett, and she swept under the wire a length ahead, in 2:20 . . ."[60]

The final heat was a nail-biter with Steve Maxwell again: "This heat was a rouser . . . Nancy Hackett was a favorite at $40 . . . The struggle was beautiful to the wire. Murphy brought his gray down kiting, passed Wolford Z. and Bonesetter, and within twenty yards of the wire was neck and neck with Nancy Hackett, when Maxwell broke, and took a run to the wire, crossing the score on even terms with the mare, but she was given the heat, in 2:21 1/4."[61]

It was the peak of the season: the celebrated horse, Rarus, had the day before at that same track set a new record of 2:13 1/4 and delighted the crowds filling the park. It was an exhibition mile, the fastest ever trotted. From the elegant ladies in the grandstand private boxes to the common young chaps wearing their best jackets down along the rail, everyone had a stopwatch to witness the thrill of the summer.

---

60 *Spirit of the Times*, August 10, 1878, <u>fultonhistory.com</u>.
61 ibid.

RARUS DRIVEN BY JOHN SPLAN ON THE COVER OF
***SPIRIT OF THE TIMES*, AUGUST 10, 1878.**

The excitement of Nancy's win rode along on the current of the midsummer Grand Circuit buzz. The newspapers listed her owners as W. C. & J. Wood, and Thomas E. Wood, the family photographer, made her picture on the occasion. The fellow in the seat of the high-wheel sulky sported a stovepipe hat and full whiskers, but his face was shadowed enough to cast into doubt his identity. Was it Hounstein? One of the Woods? John Splan drove Nancy at some point, but it wasn't clear if he was piloting her that day.[62] The petite roan mare bred and raised by the practical farmers from Tioga County was a celebrity in the newspaper. It was Nancy's moment in the sun. As *Spirit of the Times* put it, "Nancy Hackett showed herself to be a grand mare, and her performance to-day will greatly increase the fame of her sire, Wood's Hambletonian."[63]

The following week found Nancy back in Rochester for the Grand Circuit meet, where she was entered in the 2:26 class for a purse paying $1,500. It was hot and overcast on August 10, the last day of the Rochester meeting. But the wind was fierce, cutting across the track steadily all afternoon. Admission to the races was free that day, and the newspaper said the people coming in on free day were a "motley crowd."[64] The field contained most of Nancy's previous rivals and a new one: a bay gelding named Jersey Boy. Most of the horses had trouble breaking gait, and Nancy was no exception. The stiff wind and billowing dust caught the horses directly in their faces as they headed into the backstretch, knocking them off their feet. In the large field of twelve, Nancy struggled, losing her stride at least

---

62 *Utica Morning Herald*, August 17, 1878, <u>fultonhistory.com</u>.
63 August 10, 1878.
64 *Spirit of the Times*, August 17, 1878, <u>fultonhistory.com</u>

three times in the final heat and ending up in seventh place overall.[65] Jersey Boy won the last three heats and the class.

The record-breaking superstar of the year, Rarus, who had outclassed himself into exhibition status only, was also there in Rochester. He got paid a flat rate for trotting against the clock at each meet for the amazement of the crowds. But even he ran into trouble as the breeze picked up through the afternoon, slowing him on the backstretch so he could not manage to repeat his thrill from Buffalo for the Rochester crowd.

Fans were fickle as in any sporting era, and Jersey Boy was the new betting-pool favorite. The new victor of the 2:26 class boarded the railway for the next Grand Circuit venue, Utica, New York, with Nancy and the others in his wake.

As the Utica meet kicked off in the middle of August, there were about five thousand people in the stands, including, the *Spirit of the Times* happily reported, Captain Jacob Vanderbilt of New York City. Rain showers kept things soggy, but there was plenty going on— pool selling, bribery of drivers, and partying: "While the rain was coming down, and the reporters cooped up in their stand, they were courteously afforded an opportunity of drinking the health of the gallant [gelding] Hopeful (the free-for-all favorite), and his owner, Mr. A. W. Richmond, which was done with right good will."[66]

Along with Nancy and Jersey Boy, there were seven other horses in the 2:26 class, which started the afternoon of the sixteenth. The track management decided to alternate the 2:26 heats with the 2:30 class heats for that day's program, stringing it out for the entire afternoon. Jack Feek was to drive Nancy in Utica, with no clear reason as to the change. In the middle of these two classes, Rarus was

---

65 August 17, 1878.

66 *Spirit of the Times*, August 24, 1878, <u>fultonhistory.com</u>.

scheduled to trot his exhibition, which pushed things even later into the evening.

This class of horses was so evenly matched that they fought through every heat. Jersey Boy won the second, and Nancy Hackett won the fifth and sixth heat after judges substituted a stableboy for Feek amid allegations of bribery. Nancy Hackett had not been playing for a spot at the front in the first four heats, and her fans and backers complained that she had been held in. But after she got a different driver, she came on strong during the fifth heat:

"Nancy Hackett now came up from the rear, and went along very fast, passing all before her on the upper turn except Wolford Z., and at the three quarter pole she was at his throat-latch, Result lapped on the pair. The roan mare went on so fast that she took the pole at the entrance to the homestretch, and came home as an easy winner, by two lengths, in 2:20 1/4."[67]

Driver substitutions, false starts, disqualifications for breaking the gait, and other calls pushed the heats into overtime, later into the evening. The sixth heat was trotted in the dusk after 7:30 p.m. It was so dark it was hard to see the horses or tell who was breaking gait, but Nancy led off from the start and kept ahead of the rest the whole way around, winning that heat by two lengths in a time of 2:24. Nancy Hackett was *smokin'* hot. But the race had to be finished the next day.

Rarus ran into trouble that day; his driver had a disagreement with the track management about how his exhibition payment would be made. The great horse was having an off day, and there was no spectacular new record for the crowds to witness: he broke gait and

---

67 Ibid.

made a time of 2:15, a full one-and-a-half seconds slower than his grand day at Buffalo.

It rained hard again overnight, and by the morning of the seventeenth when it was time for Nancy to finish her class, the track was soft and sloppy. The race columnist for the *Utica Morning Herald* was still angry about the cheating from the previous day and aired his disgust in that morning's edition:

> If the Utica Park Association has another meeting the first hard work done should be to keep such men as "Doc" Appleberry, of Boston, and others of that gang off the track. It is men of this character that put up the jobs and tempt the drivers before races and between heats to do crooked work. Yesterday some of this gang made a powerful effort to induce Jack Feek to throw the 2:26 race with Nancy Hackett. This mare now has two heats, and can win the third and [the] race if the devils of the pool-box let her alone. We hope that the officers of the association will keep a close watch on this race today and break the back of the first man who attempts to play fraudulently.[68]

Partly due to the rainy weather and partly because it was an extra day added onto the schedule, there were barely a thousand people in the bleachers that afternoon. Nancy and her 2:26 rivals had gotten a rest, but the schemers at the betting pools had used the overnight time to their advantage as well. In the gloom after a noontime torrent of rain, the horses got the call to finish the last heats of the

---

68 *Utica Morning Herald*, August 17, 1878, <u>fultonhistory.com</u>.

race. The seventh heat was briskly contested between Jersey Boy and Nancy Hackett, the other horses well behind. At the half mile, Nancy was two lengths in the lead but broke her gait and was pulled up lame. She came in after the field and showed a badly strained hind leg, limping painfully off the track.

The next heat was thrown out because the judges suspected the other drivers were not even trying to keep up with Jersey Boy. The drivers were shuffled, each getting a different horse for the eighth heat, but there was more trouble. John Murphy, a well-known driver on the circuit, was put in for one of the drivers at the last minute but discovered that the wheels of that horse's sulky had been sprung so as to break apart during the heat. More time was spent unhitching that sulky and getting another sulky ready to go with the substitute driver. Jersey Boy finally won the ninth and last heat amid accusations of sabotage, but the judges claimed they taken measures to suppress the cheating and let the time stand. Jersey Boy's backers had made sure he won that class, one way or another. Did Nancy merely loose her footing in the mud, was she driven recklessly in the bad conditions, or had someone meddled with her shoes so as to cause her injury? While the *Spirit of the Times* hinted at fixing, the *Utica Morning Herald* writer was more adamant, reporting: "The pool box thieves would have been badly hurt had she [Nancy] won, and it is possible that there was some foul play."[69]

Later in the day a veterinary surgeon determined that Nancy Hackett's injury was permanent, as reported later in the *Spirit of the Times*: "The first heat [of that day, which was a continuation from the previous evening] was marred by a sad accident, which . . . has permanently disabled a splendid mare, Nancy Hackett."[70] She was,

---

69 *Utica Morning Herald*, August 17, 1878, <u>fultonhistory.com</u>.
70 August 24, 1878.

in the antiquated term, "stifled": the bone connecting her hip to the spine was fractured. In Utica that summer there was both mud and cheating underfoot. The crowds in the stands were heartbroken, but Nancy was the loser.

Earlier that month, the Wood brothers had been offered $5,500 for Nancy, but now her track career was over. She was given to a local fellow with the agreement that he would try to rehabilitate her to be bred. If successful, he would pay $200 for her or keep the foal. Crippled, Nancy was taken by flatboat on the Erie Canal to his home in nearby Herkimer, where she died in the fall of 1879. The documentation went silent on this point, but it seemed she suffered more than a year before she died of her ailment, or else the fellow gave up on his project and put her down.[71]

Disappointment was palpable even through a news account more than 130 years past. The sadness of Nancy's defeat just when she had a big victory in her grasp still resonated years later in 1919, when the *Utica Saturday Globe* ran a reminiscences article that highlighted the old Grand Circuit days when Utica was a major venue. Nancy's story made the paper forty years later. The Woods were fond of their horses, but as practical farmers they would have had to consider their balance sheet. Was it worth the money to ship home a crippled horse on the railway, then lay out more money trying to nurse her back to an uncertain future? Or had they sold her, or a major share in her, and had no control of her fate?[72]

Racehorse ownership had its share of fame and prestige; had the Woods tasted the seedy, gambling-driven underside as well? Perhaps they found it more comfortable to stick with the breeding business at home, remote though it was from the center of the track action

---

71 *Utica Morning Herald*, August 23, 1879, <u>fultonhistory.com</u>.
72 Ibid.

and intrigue. What Nancy achieved for the image of her sire, and for Will and Joseph Wood, was status and publicity. The small mare was one of the Woods' biggest horses. Her bright career cut short surely stung, but her name topped almost every article written about her sire or siblings down through the years. Her performance elevated the earning power of the Woods' stud: by 1882, they had a spiffy new advertising card listing the stud fee at seventy-five dollars per. In the farmers' ledger book, she fell into the column of "advertising expense." Nancy Hackett's star shone brightly on the Grand Circuit summer of 1878. They were heady days of the high-wheel sulky, when both the thrills and the gambling ran high.

Eighteen eighty-two was the year the rail line finally came up the Cowanesque Valley to change the lives of everyone, and the Woods were ready. Nancy Hackett represented the second wave of Old Dan's progeny to make it up into the Grand Circuit venues and garner headlines in the stock journals and newspapers of the time. The feisty roan mare would have plenty of company in the years to follow.

WOOD'S HAMBLETONIAN

will stand for a limited number of mares the present season, at the farm of Joseph Wood, 3 miles east of Knoxville, Tioga Co., Pa.

TERMS: $75 TO INSURE,

$25 at time of service, $50 the first of March following; in case any insured mare should not prove in foal, the $25 will apply on any mare by the same party the next season. The best of pasture provided for Mares at $2 per month. Accidents and escapes at the risk of owners.

PEDIGREE.—Wood's Hambletonian, was sired by Alexander's Abdallah, he by Rysdyk's Hambletonian; the dam of Wood's Hambletonian said to be a Morgan mare of fine style and action, and great endurance. He was bred by Dan Vansickle, of Orange Co., N. Y., (foaled 1859), who sold the colt at eight months old to O. L. Wood, from whom he derived his name; he is a dark bay roan, black points with white hind ankles, and of excellent form and trotting action, 15¾ hands high, of strong bone and muscular development; is the sire of six colts with records better than 2:30, and several others that has shown trials below 2:30; the sire of Regina, the winner of three-year-old breeder's stake, at Gentlemen's Driving Park, Morrisania, N. Y., in the time of 2:32¼.

The admirers of well-bred horses, and all persons interested in raising good stock, are respectfully invited to examine this horse. He will be allowed to serve only a limited number of Mares, and those who wish to secure his services are requested to make as early application as possible.

JOSEPH WOOD,
W. C. WOOD.

KNOXVILLE, PA., March 1, 1882.

BREEDING CARD ADVERTISEMENT. (COURTESY KNOXVILLE PUBLIC LIBRARY.)

CHAPTER 4

RAILROADS, RIVALS, AND THIEVES, 1878-1884

The disappointment of Nancy Hackett was fresh in 1878, but there was business to be attended. Her younger brother, Argonaut, was an up-and-coming star with a dollar value yet to be determined. If Will and Joseph Wood were stung by the gritty, cheating scene at the racetracks, they still had marketable livestock at home. At the Wood farm, life went on according to the seasons. Butchering hogs and hauling wood in winter gave way to spring planting. Extra mares arrived for the breeding season from May through the middle of July, followed by the summertime routine of making hay and threshing oats. Chores like milking and churning butter went on all through the year, as did caring for all animals from hens to hogs.

In any local community, the blacksmith played an important role in the culture powered by horses. Just up the road from the Wood farm next to the racetrack at Academy Corners, a blacksmith named Albert Newman (1842–1925) plied his trade.[73] A veteran of the Civil War, Newman had shod horses as he traveled and fought

---

73 Newman married a young widow with three children from Potter County whose husband, Simeon Ellis, had died in Andersonville Prison. This information was taken from the obituary of his wife, Louisa Widger Ellis Newman (Obituary, Louisa Widger Ellis Newman, unpaged clipping, Plank Scrapbook, Holbert Museum, Knoxville Public Library).

with Company L of the Second Pennsylvania Cavalry. After the war, he shod racehorses, farm horses, and even oxen. By the 1880s, oxen had fallen out of favor as the draft animal of choice, but there were still farmers and loggers who used them. Newman's price for a single horseshoe in 1879 was $0.15, or a team of two horses for $1.20. Any special shoe he made to correct a flaw in the horse's hoof cost a bit more, but Newman gave discounts to folks he knew were in difficulty. His local customers paid him by settling up a couple of times each year, often with maple sugar, potatoes, or another commodity. The visiting race men paid in cash.

Joseph Wood took Newman a wagon for repair in March of 1879 and paid him $2 for the work. The wagon was a "skeleton," a four-wheeled light rig for road racing. This scanty frame had a seat only for the driver; there was no room to take along the family. Newman also sharpened plowshares, called "colters" (his spelling), mended all manner of machinery, and made hinges and chain links.[74] A sampler of no less than sixteen styles of shoes for light (road or race) horses, nailed to a plank, remained at the Wood farm. The sampler did not include the variations of working shoes Newman would have fabricated for heavy horses, with caulks for traction to haul logs off snow-covered hillsides. It attested to the significance of the blacksmith's role in both the livelihood of farming and the sport of racing. Newman had, as a young fellow, used his skills to keep the wagons, hardware, and horses moving in the Union army. When he returned home, he made his living the same way in the era of expansion before mass-produced steel machinery changed American life.

---

74 Albert Newman blacksmith ledger 1878–1883, Knoxville Public Library, Knoxville, Pennsylvania.

C. J. Hamlin, wealthy owner of the acclaimed Village Farm in East Aurora near Buffalo, New York, paid a visit to the Wood place in Deerfield during 1881. He was seeking to buy the sire whose off-spring—such as Kilburn Jim, Nancy Hackett, and Blue Mare—had appeared on the Grand Circuit in the 1870s. His trip was chronicled in the memoirs of his farm superintendent, John Bradburn, who ac-companied him to Knoxville. When they journeyed south that year, they could ride the train only as far as the Addison, New York, sta-tion. They then had to hire a livery rig for the remaining twenty-some miles of their trip to Deerfield. Hamlin offered Joseph Wood $6,500 for Old Dan, but no sale was agreed upon. At twenty-three years of age, Dan was still sound and very popular as a stud horse, but not young. At that time, the men saw a bay mare they liked and bought her for $250.[75] Although they did not acquire the stud horse Hamlin had his eye on, he got a fast and lovely bargain in the mare who was to become known as Minnequa Maid.

Minnequa Maid's sire was, of course, Old Dan, and her dam was a mare who had come from the South during the Civil War. Tradition held that she was a Thoroughbred saddle mare captured as the mount of a Confederate officer and put in races elsewhere in Pennsylvania after the war. She then came into the hands of the Woods as a broodmare. The story of this "warhorse" mare without a name had a happier ending than that of Abdallah #15, but without more documentation it remains merely a myth.[76]

Minnequa Maid had been foaled at the Wood place in 1874, and she grew into a lovely bay mare with white hind feet and a white star on her face. Like her siblings before her, she put in training miles at the half-mile oval at Academy Corners. In 1879 she trotted a mile there at a clip of 2:24, and later in 1880 she clocked 1:10 at the half mile over the Rochester, New York, track. That day she was driven by John Halstead, a family friend from back in Orange County.

The 1887 Village Farm catalog entry for Minnequa Maid described her with an extra note: "Minnequa Maid is a very speedy mare . . ." and continued to list the mile times she had achieved, although she never seemed to trot in an official race.[77] Regardless, she earned her keep at Village Farm, and produced for Hamlin a string of successful track achievers no matter to which stallion she was bred.

---

75 John Bradburn, *Breeding and Developing the Trotter* (Boston, MA: American Horse Breeder Publishing Company, 1906), 27–28, Hathitrust Digital Library.

76 *Horse Review Portfolio*, December, 1896, unpaged, irregular publication.

77 1887 Village Farm Catalogue, East Aurora History Office.

Whether Hamlin and Bradburn discovered the mare when they came to the Woods' farm or whether they had seen her training at Rochester the previous summer with Argonaut and others and knew the pickings might be good at the Wood place was hard to tell. Hamlin and Bradburn were well-acquainted with the Woods and their horses. Bradburn was a driver from Ontario who had competed against Wood's Argonaut on the ovals of the northeast before he got hired by Hamlin around 1880. Among the anecdotes he related in his memoir, one that rang eerily familiar went as follows:

In February, 1880, I engaged to go to East Aurora, N.Y., to take charge of Mr. Hamlin's horses. At this point mention might be made of a race which did more to bring me close to Mr. Hamlin than any one thing. This was the race of August 7, 1879 in which were entered Kate Hall, Daciana, Gloster, Lady Upton, Argonaut, N----- Baby and Lady B. I was second the first and second heats with Lady Upton and thought I stood a chance to win but the owner did not want me to so I asked him to drive. After the fifth heat my mare was ruled out and the race postponed on account of darkness. The judges had not been satisfied with the way McLaughlin had driven Kate Hall, which had two heats to her credit. They took the mare away from him and placed her in charge of the police, and brought her to my stable where she remained under police protection all night. The judges asked me to drive her the next day. After I had jogged Kate Hall in the morning the judges, C. J. Hamlin, Chandler, J. Wells and Myron P. Bush, visited me and looked over the mare. They asked about her condition and I told them the mare seemed to be all right and had taken her jog work nicely. They cautioned me against having any of her harness changed and told me to be sure to drive to win, adding that if I did not the heat would be called no heat and another driver put up. I told them I would drive according to instructions. I remember Mr. Hamlin's remark: "Bradburn will win if he can; I know he will." After it became noised about that I would drive Kate Hall I was offered fifteen hundred dollars to pull the mare and lose the race. Of course I refused, although I needed the money. Another party offered me two thousand dollars to turn the same trick. I had no difficulty in winning, much to the satisfaction of Mr. Hamlin and the other judges and the owner, Mr. Hamilton. I was awarded one hundred dollars for driving.[78]

Bradburn knew his share of tricks. He often betted on horses he drove, and he could manipulate outcomes as needed, but he blamed the worst behavior on horses' owners. His own words explain more than any subsequent description could. Where were the judges—and the police—in Utica the previous summer when things went haywire for Nancy Hackett?

Not only was there cheating on the racetracks and horse thieves running roughshod over the region, there was competition for status. Whether it was gentleman's pride or a trackside squabble, the Woods had drawn the rancor of Thomas J. Berry in the village

---

78 Bradburn, *Breeding and Developing*, 15.

of Tioga. Berry was one-third owner of the other prime, Orange County–bred, pedigreed stud in Tioga County, Warwick Boy #3368. Foaled in Warwick in 1870, the colt cost so much money as a three-year-old it took three Tioga men to pool their piggy banks to bring him to Tioga. And bring him they did: Thomas J. Berry, with the Greek Revival mansion and prime land along the river on North Main Street, the banker David L. Aiken, partner in the Wickham & Aiken Bank; and tannery owner Orlando B. Lowell, who had various business ventures around that town.

Amid much fanfare, the pedigreed colt arrived in Tioga. Berry wasted no time cultivating his stallion's image in Elmira, New York, and in the regional papers and stock journals. The *Spirit of the Times* frequently ran blurbs in their horse gossip column, visiting Berry's place in 1878 and gushing about the "Horseman's Paradise" in Tioga County, Pennsylvania. Obviously patronizing his host, Berry, the columnist oozed admiration for the Berry farm and could not help a couple of grudging remarks aimed at Warwick Boy's nearest rival, Wood's Hambletonian.

On July 2, 1877, unofficial trials at Berry's Tioga track recorded a race done in three half-mile heats. One of T. J. Berry's first colts out of Warwick Boy was a chestnut gelding, Robert. In this trial, Robert bested a four-year-old colt from Wood's Hambletonian named Col. Doty. Col. Doty was bred by none other than M. D. VanScoter. VanScoter was running the Cowanesque House hotel at Academy Corners at the time, and he and O. H. were both training the horse. It was unclear which fellow had entered him in the Tioga trial. Maybe both O. H. and VanScoter were there. It was not a sanctioned race because the heats were only half the required length, but the two pals got into a disagreement with Berry that festered over the next few months.[79]

WARWICK BOY,

Brown stallion, 15¾ hands, foaled 1870, by Iron Duke, dam by Seeley's American Star; Iron Duke by Rysdyk's Hambletonian, dam by Miller's Sir Henry, second dam by Young Red Jacket, third dam by Mambrino Messenger, fourth dam by Red Bird, son of Bishop's Hambletonian; Miller's Sir Henry by Cole's Sir Henry; Duroc by Sir Henry (page 2,297); Young Red Jacket by Old Red Jacket, by Duroc (page 741); Mambrino Messenger by Mambrino, by imp. Messenger; Red Bird by Bishop's Hambletonian, by imp, Messenger.

TERMS: $50 to insure with foal.

T. J. BERRY,

975   Undercliffe Stock Farm, Tioga, Penn.

The Spirit of the Times, August 24, 1878, p. 78.

The details of their tiff were not clear, but the *Spirit* paper fed the debate with relish to keep their readers interested during the winter months when racing was quiet. Joseph Wood defended his stallion and stock with a letter to the *Spirit's* editor in February of 1878. In March of 1878, as Nancy Hackett's star rose, things were coming to a head. Berry fired back to challenge the Woods, in that paper, to a summer match in Elmira. Berry wrote a letter to the editor dated March 11, 1878, in which he expressed his insult and proposed a

---

79   Chester, *Trotting and Pacing Record*, 600.

series of match races for which he and Joseph Wood would select a colt from each year to go against the rival's colt of the same age, i.e., two-year-old against two-year-old, and the like, up to four years, and also the stallions against each other in their own race! Such a meeting would settle once and for all whose stallion was better.[80] The stallions didn't care. That several of the Woods' horses, like Nancy Hackett, had already trained at Berry's track, that some of Old Dan's daughters had been sold to Berry and bred to Warwick Boy, and that numerous Elmira horsemen, like Thomas Flood, patronized both stallions and were friends with both horsemen, was apparent. There was blending of bloodlines like a bowl of spaghetti.

Joseph Wood did not bite on the Elmira match races. It may have taken some tact to calm down O. H. and extract themselves and Dan from the quarrel, but things went quiet. O. H. Wood or VanScoter sold Col. Doty, and Berry sold Robert by September of 1878.[81]

The rivalry ended with the death of Thomas J. Berry in Elmira, New York. He died while attending the race meet there in July of 1879. He was thirty-seven years old, and left a widow and two teen-age sons.[82] By 1884, the Aiken & Wickham bank had gone into the hands of receivers, and Aiken lost his ownership share in the acclaimed stallion.

That left Lowell as the sole owner of Warwick Boy. He maintained a stable, filled with good breeding stock carrying both stallions' bloodlines, all through the decade of the 1880s. Around 1888, there were about one hundred horses at Lowell's, and he employed two trainers in addition to many other farmhand employees. He also

---

80 "A Challenge", *Spirit of the Times*, March 23, 1878, <u>fultonhistory.com</u>.
81 Ibid., 600.
82 Death notice of Thomas J. Berry, *Wellsboro Agitator*, July 10, 1879, Green Free Library Newspaper Archive.

had a herd of Jersey cattle and raised a large acreage of tobacco. Berry's racetrack along the river was still a big attraction. During these years, summer visitors swarmed in on the railways to watch their horses go that mile and filled the big hotels in town, the Park Hotel and the Brooklyn Hotel.[83]

Lowell finally dispersed his road horses at Syracuse, New York, in the Central New York Horse Breeder's Association annual sale in the spring of 1891. His horses had been left in the care of hired help who had neglected them, and they were in poor condition. Many of his broodmares sold with foals at their sides, and even the stallions went cheap. There were many of Warwick Boy's offspring among these, and a couple of mares sired by Old Dan as well.[84]

The aging stallion Warwick Boy himself was sold to Robert Urell, keeper of the Brooklyn Hotel. The financial panic of 1893 bankrupted what declining horse values had not already decimated, and the Berry track was defunct by 1894. Warwick Boy was kept by the Urell family for many more years and was photographed hitched to a wagon in front of the hotel several years later. The horse lived to a very old age, thirty-five years, and was humanely put down in 1904.[85]

Wallace's Year Book volume 6 for the year 1890 provided a snapshot comparison of the offspring of Warwick Boy with Wood's Hambletonian, as they had performed on the racetracks up to that year. For entry into the 2:30 mile list, Warwick Boy had nine offspring, while Wood's Dan listed eighteen, fully twice as many. Both stud horses lived to old age, cared for fondly by their owners in Tioga

---

83   Harry C. Kemp, *Kemp's Life Story* (New York: Carleton Press, 1960).
84   *Elmira Daily Gazette & Free Press*, May 16, 1891, <u>fultonhistory.com</u>.
85   *Elmira Telegram*, September 25, 1904, <u>fultonhistory.com</u>.

County, hours away from the center of the harness-horse sporting action.

As more of Old Dan's sons and daughters made their way into the bigger races, they sometimes faced off against each other during these years. For instance, Nancy Hackett's full younger brother Argonaut went up against another half sister, the well-known Blue Mare, in the year 1880.

According to the April 13, 1880, *Wellsboro Agitator*, the Wood Brothers sold the gelding for $5,000 to a "New Yorker" around that time. The unidentified New Yorker was the horses' regular driver, the man with many names. He turned up in news accounts with his last name spelled no less than six different ways—Horenstein, Howenstein, Hounstand, Hounstean, Hounstan, Hounstein—but his first name was always John. Hounstein entered Argonaut in several regional meets during September 1880: Cuba, Salamanca, and Dunkirk, New York. The Woods had placed Argonaut in Hounstein's care for training and traveling the previous years, and the arrangement blended owner with driver so as to make it difficult to determine when the gelding actually changed hands. Maybe the track writers and even the trotting association weren't sure who actually owned him.

Regardless, Hounstein was handling Argonaut as early as summer 1878, when the horse went into his charge at Rochester Driving Park where he was living. Argonaut made many starts during the years 1879 through 1881, but his actual ownership was sketchy: according to *Chester's Complete Trotting and Pacing Record*, J. Wood was listed as his owner when he made his record, 2:23 1/4, at Bradford,

Pennsylvania on September 17, 1880. In 1879 it seems the Woods started him in three Grand Circuit races at Buffalo, New York, on August 7 and 8, on August 12 at Rochester, New York , and Boston, Massachusetts, on September 2. Were the Woods still serious about racing a horse of their own, or were they merely keeping Argonaut, riding along on his big sister Nancy's coattails, before the public eye on the Grand Circuit to bring a nice sale price?

On August 27 of that summer, the Wood brothers put Argonaut, driven by Hounstein, in a free-for-all in the city of Dansville, New York, with his other roan half sister among his rivals. A free-for-all was a class open to both male and female horses of any age. Blue Mare had paid her share of dues over the previous years and knew her business well. That day Blue Mare made short work of that field of seven, taking all three heats.

Blue Mare deserved mention on her own merits. O. H. Wood had a favorite mare whom he called Old Bets, a daughter of the popular stud Potter's Clay. Sometime before 1870, he bred the mare to his father's up-and-coming stallion Dan. The filly O. H. got was a roan, a swirled mixture of white, gray, and black hair that when viewed from a distance appeared blue in color. O. H. started Blue Mare out on the tracks in 1874. She was neither the first nor the fastest of the Wood horses, but she paid her way over the tracks during a career that endured longer than many of her more colorful siblings. She logged thousands of miles on the railway and gave her best for at least four owners throughout her career. She was tough, she was consistent, and she was durable.

O. H.'s pal VanScoter from Hornellsville bought her at the end of the 1875 season, and he campaigned her unrelentingly during the summers of 1876 and 1877. She made her lifetime record of 2:23 at the Rochester, New York, race meet during the 1877 season. Before the season of 1878, VanScoter sold her to his friend, Hornellsville veterinarian George Williams, who ran a training stable there. Did he sell the mare in a cash transaction or trade her to pay his horse training or doctoring bill?

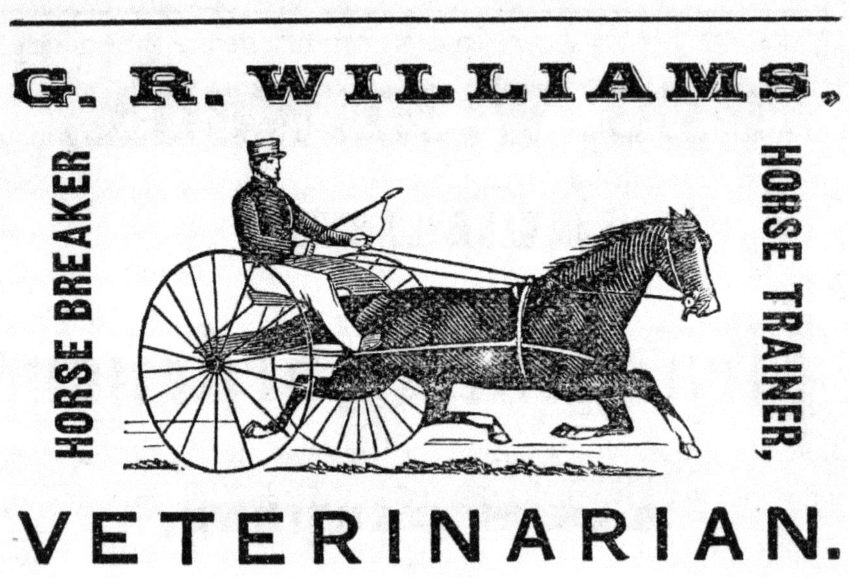

GEORGE WILLIAMS PRINT BLOCK ADVERTISEMENT.[86]
(COURTESY HORNELL PUBLIC LIBRARY).

Williams claimed her as well as her famous brother, Kilburn Jim, in a block advertisement for his veterinary and horse-training

---

86 *Smith's Hornellsville Directory 1884*, 45, Hornell Public Library.

business. Blue Mare was started by Williams in several races during 1878; then in June of the following year, Williams lost her to sheriff's sale. This meant he owed money for which his creditor filed judgment and the county sheriff seized her to satisfy the debt. A local Hornellsville doctor known as Dr. Daniel Curry bought her from the sheriff for $760. Although he did not start her in races that summer, he put her out again in 1880. After six years of steady racing, she still had what it took to dust her kid brother from Knoxville.

In 1882, another roan sister, Kitty Wood, went up against a stud colt of Dan's, her half brother named Allegany Boy #3401 (aka Allegheny Boy; there was also a later colt of the same name). Kitty Wood was bred at the Woods' Deerfield barn but foaled in Port Allegany, Pennsylvania, at the home of her dam's owner. Born in 1871, she was three years older than Allegany Boy, who was also a roan. Allegany Boy was bred at Wood's place but foaled at the farm of David Clark of Wellsboro, Pennsylvania, in 1874. The spotted siblings earned their way to the Grand Circuit Buffalo meeting on August 3, 1882, where they trotted in the same 2:33 class with four others. That day Allegany Boy got fourth money, and his sister placed just below him but got no payoff. Kitty Wood would earn her record time—a respectable 2:24 1/4— a couple of years later in July of 1885.[87]

Allegany Boy had to contend with yet another sister the next summer. Sibling rivalry played out on the racecourse as both colts were gifted with the same genetics and speed. This gal—named Kit Sanford—was a beautiful, wiry bay just one year older than himself. Foaled in the Cameron County, Pennsylvania, lumber village of Emporium, she had a racehorse for a dam as well. Kit had made

---

87 *New York Herald*, August 4, 1882, <u>fultonhistory.com</u>.

herself known as a force to be reckoned with on the racing circuit beginning in 1880, and in Dunkirk, New York, on June 19, 1883, she met Allegany Boy in the 2:33 class for a $500 purse. She took all three heats and beat her brother in each one. They placed first and second money that day.

Kit was always popular with track writers and was sold early in her life to George W. Murray of Bath, New York, who had her professionally trained and driven by Charles Sherman of Penn Yan, New York. Often referred to as the Sanford mare, she held up well over the next several years, earning her fastest record time of 2:21 1/4 at Rochester in August of 1885. Kit changed hands several times and was retired from the racetrack to become a broodmare. She appeared last in the papers as a bred mare consigned in a sale of high-bred trotting stock in Lexington, Kentucky, in 1888.[88]

There were Dan's own stud colts in the region also. It seemed there was a gentlemen's understanding that owners of ungelded sons of Old Dan would set up for breeding business at a respectable distance so as not to undercut his rising stud fees.

Sons of Dan, most of them carrying a variation of his name, advertised during these years included the following:

- Fleetwood, advertised in 1879 in Woodhull, New York
- Hambletonian Dan, Jr., advertised in 1879 in Wellsboro, Pennsylvania
- Newcomb colt, Argo A. #9172, advertised in 1887 in Nelson, Pennsylvania
- Daniel Lee, advertised in 1888 in Cuba, New York
- Halwood, advertised in 1892 in Brookfield, New York

---

88 *Spirit of the Times*, January 28, 1888, fultonhistory.com.

There were most certainly others scattered around the region as well, their stud fees around $10 making them more affordable to farmers than the $75–$100 range that racing studs fetched during the same years. It was common for crossbred stallions in this price range to travel a set route during the breeding season; the owners would advertise the days of the week the stallion would be at such-and-such location, often a blacksmith shop or a hotel livery barn. Farmers would know where to take their mares on which day. Neither Oliver Wood nor Will and Joseph were found to have taken Dan off their farm for breeding. It was said that the stallion seldom left the place. Of two occasions on which he supposedly did, neither could be corroborated from secondary sources. One news writer later wrote of Dan that "Mr. Wood would never let him be taken away from home . . ."[89] Whether this referred to father Oliver or son Joseph is not clear.

These sons of Old Dan did not trot at sanctioned meets, they were not registered as Standardbreds because their frugal owners did not want to spend the extra cash to send in the paperwork, or they were heavy because their dams were draft mares. These stallions were serving the dual-purpose market for farmers and lumbermen as well as buggy horses. Farmers liked the Norman—what is now referred to as Percheron—horses for brute strength, but heavy horses were expensive to feed. Logging photographs revealed that many of these animals were rangy yet not carrying the bulk of modern Percherons and Belgians. The draft breeds of Britain were not popular in the region, and the Belgian types had not yet been introduced.

Fast road horses were a thrill, but the reality of life here was profoundly practical. Plenty of folks thought horse racing was frivolous or morally wrong due to the gambling aura which surrounded it.

---

89 "Spotted Sam's Relatives," *The Trotter and the Pacer*, April 17, 1930, mi-harness.net.

Most working men needed a horse who could haul logs all winter, plow and rake hay in the summer, take the family visiting on Sunday, and not eat them out of house and home. Some of these fellows, it appeared from the advertisements, were exactly that: they possessed the snazzy speed from Old Dan, but their dams were hefty Norman-cross gals who endowed them with larger frames and bulk for the grunt work of the timbered hillsides.

Crossbreds had another advantage for the farmers as well. Temperament was an issue. Lumbermen and farmers depended on steady horses who wouldn't spook or take off. Foal handling and training was crucial, but all horsemen knew that individuals of the racing bloodlines had trouble settling down, meaning they were high-strung or feisty sometimes.

But how far away was courteous noncompetition? If Joseph and Will preferred their competition at arms' length, that did not stop brother O. H. and his son-in-law, Jerome Hathaway, from their own aspirations. Of the Wood family horsemen, O. H. had the strongest affinity for fast horses, and he put up a competing stud horse closer to home than anyone else. Kinfolk rivalry may have been polite, but it was real nonetheless. By the late 1870s, it seemed that O. H. had given up his expectation of owning Dan. He took his favorite mare, good Old Bets, to Daniel Sayer back in Orange County and ended up with a strong stud colt whom he named Wood's Guy Miller. The horse's sire, Sayer's Guy Miller #861, was owned by two Unionville brothers-in-law long known to the Wood family: Daniel Sayer and John Halstead. Sayer may have been related to the Woods by marriage; Halstead was a farmer who sold insurance and trained horses for the Woods at several locations from Academy Corners to Buffalo. Halstead was tight with both generations of Woods, having acted as witness for Oliver's will and erstwhile race trainer for his sons. Like the stud O. H.'s father brought and his brothers now owned, his stallion shared the same grandsire, good old Rysdyk's Hambletonian #10. This stud he advertised in the *Knoxville Courier* in May of 1883.

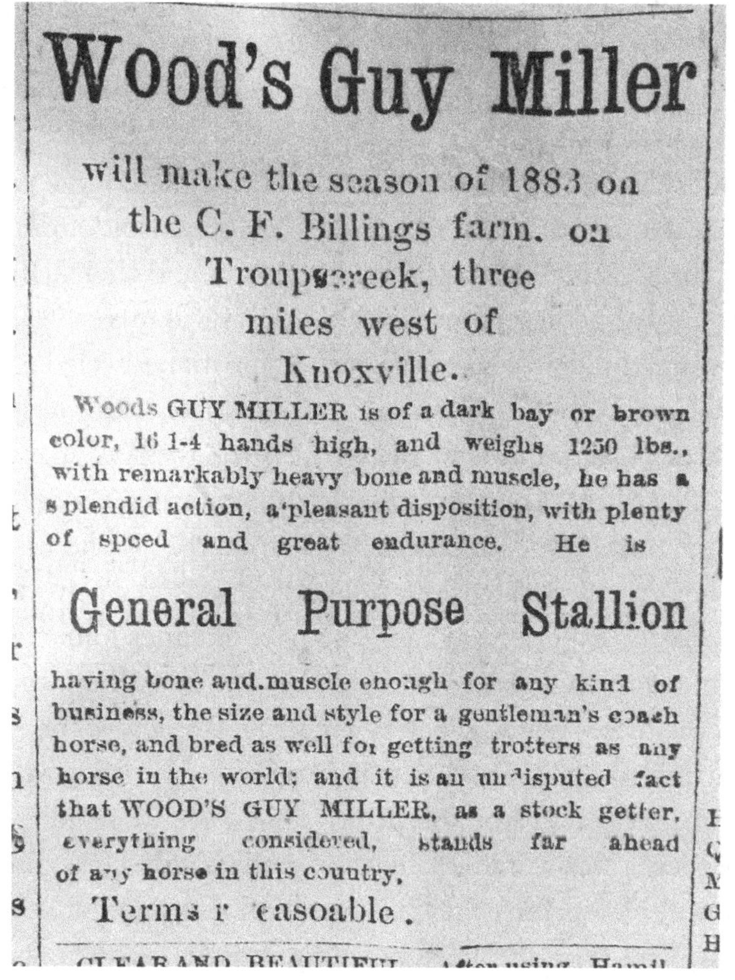

O. H. Wood stallion advertisement for Woods' Guy Miller, Knoxville Courier, May 26, 1883.

The horse was stabled at the farm of Charles F. Billings, up the Austinburg road, three miles north of Knoxville. The ad offered no pedigree but asserted bold claims, with O.H.'s brothers and their family's stallion just down the road. There was no set price listed.

The following year, the stallion suffered a fracture and had to be put down: "A stallion known as 'Wood's Guy Miller,' belonging to Wood & Hathaway, of Knoxville, had its leg broken by a kick from another horse, a few days ago, resulting in the death of the animal. It was valued at $5,000."[90]

Stallions would fight, so horsemen built stalls and paddocks stoutly as to prevent such an accident to a valuable animal. The breeding process could pose danger to horses and their handlers as well. Owners of pedigreed mares did not want to miss a year of that mare's production. No foal, no money. Some mares cycled regularly, but others would show no obvious heat and were tricky to get bred. With mares' gestation taking a lengthy eleven months, many horsemen considered that the most reliable time to breed a mare was her "foal heat," nine days after she had given birth.[91] If the mare traveled for her breeding date, she would arrive with her new foal at her side. It took the experienced handling of sometimes four men to see to each horse in this process: one to handle the stallion, one at the halter of the teaser gelding, one to keep a jumpy new foal nearby but out of harm's way, and another to see to the jittery mare who wasn't happy to be separated from her foal.

Whether it was a stallion fight or a mishandled breeding, their horse was dead. Luckily, they had a colt all ready to put up in their stallion's niche. For the next breeding season in 1885, they were ready to go with another stud horse, a splendid son of Wood's Guy

---

90 *Addison Advertiser*, May 22, 1884, <u>fultonhistory.com</u>.

91 J. H. Sanders, *Horse Breeding: Being the General Principles of Heredity Applied to the Business of Breeding Horses, with Instructions for the Management of Stallions, Brood Mares and Young Foals, and the Selection of Breeding Stock* (Chicago: Illinois, J.H. Sanders Pub. Co., 1888),151-155,170, Hathitrust Digital Library.

Miller, with a most original name: Hathaway's Guy Miller. Neither of these stud horses had a registry number, so they likely did not court the racing clientele.

For the 1885 breeding season, you could take one mare to the Hathaway horse for $10 or two mares for the bargain price of $16. The advertisement stated that he had bred mares in Bath and Hornellsville, New York, had worked in the lumber woods during the winter of 1881, and had trotted a road mile in 2:50. Not a bad time for a heavy fellow. A couple of years later, Hathaway had a man take his versatile stallion on a weekly tour for his breeding season, making a circuit from Knoxville, Little Marsh, Westfield, and Harrison Valley to Whites Corners and back. If you did not aspire to race, this well-rounded fellow was, at $10, much more within the farmer's budget. If the Wood brothers gathered the family at Christmas time, they must have had plenty of horseflesh to chat about.

There was no shortage of drama in the Cowanesque Valley during the years between Nancy Hackett and Mamie Wood.[92] Horse thieves were afoot. Joseph Wood eschewed advertising in the paper, but he had a point to make when he paid for a block ad in the column of the *Wellsboro Agitator* on June 21, 1881, giving notice of a missing mare: "STRAYED OR STOLEN.—Disappeared from the pasture of the subscriber, about four weeks ago, a brown mare, 3 years old, with heavy mane and tail, sloping rump, about 15 1/2 hands high, very little white in the forehead, right hind foot white. I will pay a

____

92 This mare was referred to in print as both Mamie Wood and Mamie Woods. She was the same horse.

liberal reward for the return of the colt or knowledge of its where-abouts. JOSEPH WOOD, Knoxville, Tioga County, Pa."[93]

He had already searched for four weeks, and his neighbors were familiar with his stock. He knew the filly had not wandered off, and he was putting the region on notice that folks were on the lookout for her.

Horse thievery was a widespread problem. A notice in the Westfield paper of the same year described a watchdog group over several counties whose express purpose was to cut down on the crime of horse theft: "A vigilance association for the prevention of horse stealing is being organized to extend over the mountains of Steuben, Chemung, and Tioga, N.Y., and Tioga, Bradford, and Potter Counties in Pennsylvania. This association proposes to find the horses stolen or reimburse the owners in about two-thirds of their loss."[94]

Local sheriffs notwithstanding, the horsemen were looking out for their own interests with a private-subscription style of law en-forcement. Whether Joseph had a part in this endeavor or whether he ever recovered his missing filly is not known, but his farm and his stud's offspring were located dead center of this region. Allegany County, with its popular racetracks in Cuba, Scio, and Wellsville, was, interestingly, not included.

Fast horses bred at the Woods' place trotted at their home coun-ty seat of Wellsboro, Pennsylvania also. The racecourse had two dis-tinct lives; oval at one time but widened at one end later, so as to be kite-shaped. The footprint of the track location along Nichols Street

---

93 Green Free Library Newspaper Archive.

94 Undated, unidentified newsprint clipping, likely *Westfield Courier*, Westfield, Pennsylvania, Plank Scrapbook, Holbert Museum, Knoxville Public Library.

is viewable in the 1875 Beers atlas, and is also visible in the large framed map on display at Green Free Library in Wellsboro.

A bit of racetrack rivalry played out in the southern towns of the county during the mid-1880s as well. R. M. Ketcham had a livery stable in downtown Wellsboro and drove a fast, competitive gelding named Dutchman, not from Old Dan. Stephen F. Richards from Covington owned a roan colt he had bred from Old Dan in Knoxville whom he called Bucephalus (Alexander the Great's famous mount). Bucephalus was an outsized fellow; his dam was Richards' Percheron cross mare. In August 1886, Ketcham took his pride and joy, Dutchman, south to Covington. In the free-for-all there, Bucephalus took first place, a mare Daisy B. took second, but Ketcham's Dutchman came in a closely-contested third.[95] When Richards did not show up the following week at Wellsboro with Bucephalus for another crack at Dutchman in his hometown, Ketcham wasn't happy. Even though Dutchman beat Daisy in the 2:32 class and both his trotting mares did well at that meet, Ketcham still wanted a piece of Bucephalus:

"Many of our horsemen went to the Covington races the previous Saturday with the explicit understanding that the Covington horses should participate in the races here. But none of them appeared. The following card has been handed to us for publication.

There seems to be a great feeling in regard to the Richards stallion, inasmuch as he did not put in an appearance on Saturday, August 28th, to compete with Dutchman and Daisy B., as agreed upon by his owner therefore Mr. R. M. Ketcham challenges Mr. S. F. Richards to trot his roan stallion against his black gelding, Dutchman, in a race, best three in five, for from one to five hundred dollars a side,

---

95 *Wellsboro Agitator*, August 24, 1886. Green Free Library News Archive.

over the Wellsboro track, at any time within four weeks after the third day of September next. If this challenge is accepted, articles of agreement shall be drawn up and date named for the race and a forfeit of $50 deposited at time of making agreement. R. M. Ketcham"[96]

Richards did not take Bucephalus back to trot against the irate Wellsboro folks. Instead, he took him to Mansfield to the fair in October. "Mr. S. F. Richards, of Covington, carried off numerous first premiums on his Hambletonians, beginning with the handsome stallion, Bucephalus, and ending with a two-year-old as pretty as a picture."[97]No race here, just judging for premiums.

The following fall at the Mansfield Fair there were, among others in the stallion judging classes, two horse colts sired by Bucephalus. Richards, however, never sent in registration papers for Bucephalus. The stallion was not registered until 1892, when his then-owner, named T.C. Peck, submitted his pedigree and papers. He was finally official: Bucephalus #14554.[98]

Eighteen eighty was the year that Joseph Wood bought out his brother William's share in the farm, and their aged parents, Oliver L. and Thankful, divested themselves of their remaining property in Deerfield and returned to Unionville, New York. Why the older couple returned was not revealed; it can only be guessed that it had to do with children in both places. The sons and their families were in the new home, yet two of the daughters had stayed in the old home area. The farm in Minisink had not been sold, only rented, so the ties remained. Father Oliver L. died at the home of Sam and Emily Christie in 1882, and Thankful died in 1884. Both were laid

---

96 "The Races Last Saturday", *Wellsboro Agitator*, August 31, 1886. Green Free Library News Archive.

97 *Wellsboro Agitator*, October 5, 1886. Green Free Library News Archive.

98 *Wallace's American Trotting Register*, v.10, 1892, 57, Hathitrust Digital Library.

to rest in Unionville. Their offspring who came to Pennsylvania did not return for burial there, however. If the story of migratory people was told in the place they chose to rest for the ages, then it occurred in the Wood family with Joseph's generation.

How the ownership of Old Dan was transferred was also lost to time. Was he a gift or a carefully valued asset sold from father to sons? Because the stallion was not listed separately on Oliver L.'s estate inventory after his death in 1882, Old Dan was not inherited as per the definition. Certainly both William and Joseph were involved in the breeding operation, but whether they were co-owners of the stud horse or merely worked together is not clear. Will did not marry until 1877, when at the age of forty-two he took young Nannie Ray as his bride. She was about twenty years his junior, with curls and apple cheeks. Her father, Nelson G. Ray, was a horseman pal of the Woods. It was at his farm just south of the Cowanesque River at Academy Corners where Will and Nannie set up housekeeping. Will had moved about a mile from Joseph's place. In 1880, William deeded his share of the main 220-acre farm to Joseph and his wife, Myrtilla. Joseph's first two sons, Fred and Perry, were youngsters born in 1871 and 1875, respectively, but the later children were yet to arrive on the scene.

The year 1880 stood as a benchmark in another aspect, because the federal agricultural census taken that year provided an itemized picture of the Woods' farm. Taken each decade, the census offered a view of the crops, livestock, and farm output in that particular year. Only a few of these were extant for Pennsylvania, and that year's record was one of those rare gems. Joseph Wood listed himself as owner of the farm and valued his livestock together at $12,500. The stud was not listed separately but included in eighteen horses listed, with a few head of "milch" cows, calves, sheep, a couple of pigs, and a small flock of twenty chickens. It was a typical diversified farm for the time, making butter and honey for sale and growing a variety of crops for the family's use and for sale. Apple trees were listed, as well as corn, oats, wheat, and potatoes.[99]

For the local tax assessment of 1880, however, the brothers Joseph and W. C. were listed in a joint entry for the 220-acre farm. Together they claimed only six horses in addition to the stallion, who was valued at $400. Their brother O. H. listed 240 acres but no livestock, while elder brother A. S. claimed a farm of 142 acres, one horse, and thirteen dairy cows. In 1883, Old Dan was listed in the brothers' joint entry valued at $1,200.[100] This after Joseph had refused Hamlin's offer of $6,500 for him in the interval. For the well-heeled customer, the stud horse was worth much more than for the tax man.

The census revealed that Will Wood owned his farm separately that year, and though he listed diverse crops and livestock as well, he reported fourteen horses without indicating where those horses were stabled. It was possible that some of those horses were mingled with Joseph's.

Joseph Wood owned a few broodmares of his own, gals who called the place home and dropped Old Dan's foals each year. Mares such as Belle were likely included in the horse number, along with young stock like three young colts such as Linden S. #6412, Pactolus B. #6413, and Davie C. #6414, for whom Joseph Wood sent in

---

99 National Archives, Washington; Record Group 029, National Archives and Records Service, General Services Administration; Federal Decennial Census, 1880, *Tioga County, Deerfield Township*, pp. 8-11, lines 2-7, www.phmc.pa.state.us.

100 Township of Deerfield Local Tax Assessment for the Years 1880 and 1883, print copy, Knoxville Public Library.

registration papers.[101] Could these have been the roans Harry Kemp drove in his 1890 brush on the Barney Hill Road?

One of the best broodmares on the Wood place was a gal with a Morgan Black Hawk pedigree whom they called simply May. They bought her in Ithaca, New York, as a young mare, and her first foal for Woods was the roan colt, Achates #12763, in 1877. He was sold to a buyer in Conneat, Ohio. It was possible he may have been the horse young Perry delivered on the train from the oral story carried down through that family branch.

May's fillies, named Meryl and Myrtie, were bought in 1881 by C. J. Hamlin and taken to Village Farm to become broodmares there. May's best track performer was her 1880 daughter, Elda B., who as a mare got no registry number. Elda had many wins at Grand Circuit and smaller, regional tracks during the years 1887 through 1890, and her record mile stood at a respectable 2:20 1/2.

FOR SALE.

A FIVE-YEAR-OLD STALLION, standard bred. by Wood's Hambletonian. No. 572 (sire of Nancy Hackett, record 2:20; Mamie Wood, two-year-old record 2:27¼, and fourteen others with records below 2:30); dam by Dandy (son of Black Hawk, No. 21. Stands 16 hands high and weighs 1,150 lbs.; is a beautiful bay, with black points and a very heavy tail; is kind and gentle, and a fine road horse; has never been trained and is a sure foal getter.

For terms and further particulars address

W. A. NEWCOMB,

Nelson, Tioga County, Pa.

CAPTION: WELLINGTON NEWCOMB KEPT THE HOTEL IN OLD NELSON, AND PUT ARGO A. #9172 IN RACES AT WELLSBORO, PENNSYLVANIA DURING THE 1880s. THE STALLION WAS LATER OWNED BY ROSS LEACH AT THE LIVERY OF SMITH HOTEL IN WESTFIELD IN 1899.

---

101 *Wallace's American Trotting Register*, vol. 7, 1887, Hathitrust Digital Library.

In 1882, May produced a bay colt, Argo A. #9172, who was sold to Wellington A. Newcomb, who kept the hotel and livery stable in Nelson. The village of Nelson was just a few miles east on the river road along the Cowanesque. She followed these with more bay colts, Albert W. #10071 in 1884 and Gilbert S. #10392 in 1885. During the mid-1880s, the barn was full of young trotting stock, many of them roans. With offspring of Old Dan coming into Grand Circuit success during these years, the Woods could anticipate selling these colts for good prices. They were already registered with the National Association of Trotting Horse Breeders and not gelded, to maximize their potential for future earnings if they panned out on the track.

Shortly after 1880, the Woods began to cultivate tobacco along with many of their neighbors in the Cowanesque Valley. This cool-season variety of Connecticut broadleaf was labor intensive, well suited to the loamy river bottom flats, and returned a good profit in the late 1800s. Tobacco took an important role in the farm economy of the region. Its rise and fall virtually paralleled the peak of the trotting horses in the region as well.[102]

As for the local racetrack at Academy Corners, it was to be sacrificed for the new railroads. Two competing lines, the Addison & Northern Pennsylvania Railroad Company and the Corning, Cowanesque & Antrim Railway Corporation, were scrambling to lay claim up the valley. Extending their lines westward from Elkland toward Potter County, these would in the years to follow become known as the Baltimore & Ohio and the New York Central. By 1881, the rights of way for both rail lines were marked directly across the driving park, carving it into three separate pieces. The rival companies had no intention of sharing the profits they envisioned from

---

102   Paul O'Rourke, et al, *From Buckskin to Baseball: Glimpses of Tiogans at Work and Play,*(Wellsboro, Pa.:, Tioga County Historical Society, 1978) 53.

access to the tanneries and lumber mills farther west. The two lines ran parallel across the fertile river farmlands of the Wood farm as well, crossing it in not one but two places, just a few hundred feet apart.

During 1882, both companies scurried along, grading and laying rails westward up the Cowanesque Valley. On the one hand, the local horsemen and farmers were gaining better access to markets and passenger service to cities, but they had to give up Knoxville's local horse track in the name of progress. Though everyone was to benefit from the new railroad—think high-speed internet of recent years—the Knoxville group of horsemen did not build another track there. It would be several years until a Westfield group calling itself the Agricultural Society would acquire land west of town at the junction of the main road with North Fork Road. The society would build a racetrack there in connection with their fair, which made its debut in September 1887.[103]

Other events were occurring in Deerfield Township at this time, when natural resources seemed limitless, forest management was not yet even a concept, and the pollution of streams with tannery waste was common. Lumber was in high demand, tanneries needed hemlock bark, coke ovens needed coal, and railroads hustled to haul it all out. The decade of the 1880s saw the opportunity and the demise of Pennsylvania's forest: sawmills buzzed and business boomed. No wonder there were terrible floods in 1889 and 1916, there was little vegetation to stop the erosion of the clear-cut hillsides. Bobcats, lynx, deer, and bear disappeared. Mountain farms were cleared, though many were worked only a generation before they went broke and reverted to woodland. In 1882, the mines of Fall Brook, Antrim,

---

103 *Wellsboro Agitator*, October 9, 1888, Green Free Library Newspaper Archive.

and Arnot were going full speed, the railways bustled to ship out the coal, and telegraph lines carried news along the route.[104] Immigrants, many from Eastern Europe, populated the coal villages. The forest landscape was transformed, with only the cautionary voices of Muir, Nessmuk, and Thoreau too late in its defense. The Barnhart log loader and Shay locomotive were to the Pennsylvania timberlands what hydraulic fracturing is to shale gas now: the technology that allowed the final, complete extraction of the natural resource. The last steep slopes of the state's vast stands of trees were turned into cash between 1880 and 1910.[105]

---

104 *Wellsboro Agitator*, January 3, 1882. Green Free Library News Archive.
105 Thomas T. Taber, III, *Logging Railroad Era of Lumbering in Pennsylvania*, vols. 4 & 7,(Williamsport, PA.: Lycoming Printing Company), 1972, 1975.

CHAPTER 5

MAMIE WOOD: PRIDE AND POLITICS

It was late summer in 1883, well after the usual breeding season, that Elmira pharmacist Thomas S. Flood (1844–1908) made arrangements for his favorite mare to travel to Joseph Wood's farm. He likely cabled his request or simply telegraphed what date and time the mare was expected at the brand-new Knoxville rail station. Her name was Mary Ann, and she was as beautiful as she was well-bred. Flood had brought several mares to Joseph Wood during the previous years, and by that year he had more than one youngster in his stables sired by Old Dan.

Thomas Flood was a popular member of the prominent family of Floods whose several homes occupied an entire residential block in Elmira. His father and brothers were doctors, and Flood augmented the medical tradition in the family with his drugstore on East Water Street. Born along Seneca Lake in Lodi, New York, Flood went to medical school like his father and brothers, but instead of practicing medicine he chose pharmacy as his career.

HON. THOMAS S. FLOOD, CHEMUNG COUNTY HISTORICAL
SOCIETY, ELMIRA, NEW YORK. (USED WITH PERMISSION.)

Flood had a strong affinity for horses, and he soon had a barnful in the city. Shortly after his marriage in 1870 to a young lady named Frances Miller, for whose family Miller Street on the south side of that city was named, her uncle John E. DuBois recruited Flood into his plans for the lumber trade. DuBois the younger (son of the Williamsport lumber baron by the same name for whom the Duboistown neighborhood of that city was named) had purchased more than thirty thousand acres of timber, mostly white pine, in western Pennsylvania. It was then a veritable wilderness.

DuBois engaged Flood to move out to Clearfield County, Pennsylvania, and help manage the lumber takings: mills, railroad lines, labor force, housing, post office, and the like. There were few constraints on industry in that era, and the settlement was part of the ever-moving western line of America's woodlands that at the time appeared to have no end. The town became known as DuBois. Uncle DuBois was the capital and oversight behind the building of the town, and Flood was one of several men who made it happen. White pine was cash, and Flood's wealth was secured during that decade, by 1880.[106]

Joseph Wood and Thomas Flood were contemporaries whose business relationship through horses continued for many years. Though they occupied different places on the social and economic scale, the duration of the horse breeding and selling transactions indicated the respect each shared for the other's role within horse racing. Thomas Flood was two years older than Joseph Wood, and they each got married in 1870. By 1880, each was settling into his vocation, Flood's early chapter in DuBois having secured him financially for his next step: politics.

---

106 *Elmira Advertiser*, "Hon. Thomas Flood Passed Away in Pittsburg Last Night," October 29, 1908,Chemung County Historical Society, Booth Library.

With his wife, Frances, young son, Chester, and his contingent of horses, Flood returned to the family seat in Elmira. At the time, Flood's father, Dr. Patrick Flood and his two brothers and their families occupied several homes situated on the block along East Water Street between DeWitt Avenue and Madison Avenue. Carriage houses and horse barns were also situated on these grounds held by the extended Flood family. This block adjacent to St. Joseph's hospital is now occupied by the red brick Church of God, two older residential buildings at the rear, and the public housing complex George Bragg Towers with its parking lots along East Water Street.

Flood resumed his drugstore business and ran for city alderman in 1882, and surprised everyone when he won as a Republican in a Democratic ward. He also got involved with showing and racing his horses in the Chemung County Agricultural Society, the predecessor to the Chemung County Fair. Holding office with the society, Flood applied his business acumen to his political and equine pursuits. A popular guy, he was known to be fair in the show ring and fast on the track.

Flood had owned the beautiful bay mare Mary Ann since 1874, when he lived in DuBois. A daughter of the pedigreed trotting stallion Magnolia #68 (by Seely's American Star #14),[107] she was a seasoned mother, having produced six foals for Flood. Flood and other Elmira horsemen had beaten a path to Joseph Wood's farm during the previous decade. Drawn by the Grand Circuit success of Kilburn Jim, Nancy Hackett, and others, there had been several Elmira horsemen who trotted their mares on the dirt roads about forty miles to Wood's stud horse before there were rails to ride.

---

107 Wallace, *Year Book*, vol. 7.

The road between Knoxville and Elmira ran both ways. Wood had a couple of broodmares sired by Flood's stallion, Magnolia #68, as well. They either bought the mares from Flood or sent mares of their own to Flood as a trade of stud services. A roan colt, registered by Joseph Wood with the name of Linden S. #6412, was foaled in Wood's Knoxville barn in 1885, a son of Old Dan. But Linden's dam, owned by Joseph Wood, was sired by Magnolia.[108] That Woods purchased pedigreed mares, like May from Ithaca, and got mares by other notable trotting stallions into their lot of broodmares showed that for a time, at least, they were actively breeding for the market themselves. While not on the scale of Hamlin in Buffalo or Wilson in Kentucky, they produced and sold young racing stock of their own in the 1880s.

Mary Ann's first visit to Old Dan had been in 1877; she gave birth to the bay filly Regina in 1878. Why did Flood bring Mary Ann back to Knoxville after a gap of several years? Her fast daughter Regina, foaled in 1878, had only begun to show off her talents at the track during 1881 as a three-year-old. It took almost four years to see what the breeding of the two pedigrees could attain. If the match had produced something so lovely—and so lucrative—once, it was worth another try.

The Wood Brothers used Regina's achievement to the fullest, emblazoning her record, "Fastest three year old outside of California," on their new advertising card in 1882.

Mamie Wood was foaled in the summer of 1884, a fine filly whose roan coloring from her sire became apparent as she grew. Her parentage and her older siblings were well-known, and Flood had big expectations for Mamie. It was an exciting year for the Floods, as

---

108   See chapter 4 for the first mention of Linden S.

they had a new baby girl born as well. They named their new daughter Frances Mabel, after her mother, but called her Mabel. Their son, Chester, was now about seven years old.

By this time, Flood had moved his horses from East Water Street out to an expansive 185-acre spread he'd acquired south of Elmira over the state line in the Bradford County village of Fassett, Pennsylvania. The place was traditionally known as the Philo Fassett House, and its location was about halfway along the road south to Troy, Pennsylvania, from Elmira. During the stagecoach days, it had been operated as an inn with a livery stable. Flood gave the place a new name, Magnolia Stock Farm, after the stallion whose genetics ran in several of his broodmares, among them Mary Ann. Flood could catch the railway south from the city and be at his farm in only a few minutes, riding the line known first as the Williamsport & Elmira Railroad. Later it became known as the Northern Central, and the road down the valley is now Route 14. The place was near the church in the village, and according to one source he built his own training track across the road from the house.[109] Only his horses lived in Fassett; he and his family lived in the city.

The number of horses Flood stabled at Magnolia Stock Farm differed between sources. Some newspapers claimed that he had as many as thirty-five horses there, but his property tax records reported eight at most during the peak years of the mid-1880s.[110] The truth was likely somewhere in between; one low-balled things when the assessor came around. Flood kept dairy cows at the barns there

---

109   Edward P. Ballard, et al, *South Creek Township Sesquicentennial,1833-1983*,35,Bradford County Historical Society.

110   South Creek Township real property tax rolls, 1882–1906, Bradford County Historical Society.

as well, and hired a man to live there and look after things during his long absences for business and legislative sessions.

Flood showed Mamie off to a writer for the *Spirit* in July of 1885, when she was a yearling in the pasture. In an article praising the offspring of Mary Ann at Magnolia Farm, the columnist gushed:

> But evidently the idol of Mr. Flood is the youngest of the brood, Mamie Woods, full sister to Regina. For purity of action and conformation, probably this filly is unsurpassed by any yearling trotter in the State. At least this is the conviction of half a score of intelligent horsemen who recently saw her taken from pasture, and led beside a runner from wire to wire, a half mile, in 1:36, and with her halter-strap leading from her head back to the rider's hand the whole distance. She is entered in the Matron Stakes for 1887, also in other stake events to be trotted in her two and three year old form. She will be broken to harness this fall, and, if no mishap befalls her, there will be a two-year-old race-horse next season.[111]

At the Wood homestead in the Cowanesque Valley that year, Joseph Wood was building a fine new house for his growing family. The old, plain farmhouse was moved many yards off the old foundation, while the lovely new structure took shape on its site. It featured a beautiful hardwood banister in the front hall, large heavy-paneled pocket doors, laundry chutes, and other amenities of the time. It was Victorian fancy, with exterior gingerbread fretwork at the gables,

---

111 *Spirit of the Times*, July 18, 1885, <u>fultonhistory.com</u>.

window sashes, and porches. A grand lady of the Valley, it bore witness to the Woods' pride in their horses and their farm.

Wood home built in **1885**.

At Magnolia Farm in Fassett, Mamie started her training in harness during the years of 1885 and 1886, under the hand of Flood's trainer, John Ryan. Flood was very pleased with her prospects. According to his plans, she was to make her debut as a two-year-old in the New York State Breeders' Association meet in September of 1886. Just to get some experience, Mamie trotted an exhibition at the Maple Avenue Driving Park in Elmira on June 3, going one mile alone against the stopwatch in 2:44 1/2.[112]

The breeders' meeting at Rochester, New York, was open to the public but designed to let the horsemen test each other's stock within their membership. At this meet there were stakes races, where the members sponsored classes for foals born in the same year, or

---

112 John Hankins Wallace, *Wallace's Year-Book of Trotting and Pacing in 1886*, vol. 2, 12, Hathitrust Digital Library.

four-year-old stallions against each other, and the like. It did not draw the same kind of crowds and betting that the Grand Circuit races did, but the goal was comparison between breeding programs. Hamlins from Buffalo wielded a large presence so close to their home turf. C. J. Hamlin's favorites, like Belle Hamlin and Justina, were on hand with others from Village Farm. Along with Mamie, Flood took with him another colt from Elmira, her half brother, Floodwood, born the year before and also sired by Old Dan. Mamie was entered in the No. 2 Dreamland Stake, for foals born in 1884.

On Tuesday, Sept. 7, 1886, with the other colts drawn (withdrawn or scratched), she went up against one other horse for the stake. She easily distanced her competitor during the first heat and was award-ed the stake, with a time of 2:31 1/2 recorded. It was considered a good mile time for a two-year-old, but Flood had bigger fish to fry: he wanted to see—or maybe his friends challenged him, over a bot-tle of scotch, to prove—whether Mamie could break the record for two-year-olds. It was a publicity event, aimed squarely at that other stronghold of breeding: Kentucky. The fastest time for a two-year-old had been made the previous year by a (Kentucky) gelding named Nutbreaker, son of the esteemed and prolific stud, Nutwood #600, a Kentucky native who went to Pennsylvania, California, and back.

So two days later as the wind blew briskly and the temperature hovered around forty degrees, Mamie appeared for her exhibi-tion. Nutbreaker was four states away. She would trot against the clock, with a companion horse to provide competitive conditioning. Horses trotted faster when they had other horses to go against, "in company," as they called it in those days. Mamie was still a young filly. Though the crowd was sparse and most of the ladies stayed home due to the chill, Flood drove Mamie out on the track to do her best. He had something to prove to his friends and colleagues, and whether it was building lumber mills in the wilderness of DuBois or debating Elmira's city issues, he was used to pushing ahead for what he wanted.

The *Rochester Democrat and Chronicle* reported the attempt:

> The event of the day was Mamie Woods' [sic] endeavor to break the best two-year-old record of 2:29. She was first sent a slow mile, finishing in 2:43 1/4. When she came on the track again she was accompanied by a pacer. Both came under the wire together, but Mamie began to go ahead, the pacer not seeming to follow her pace. The first quarter was made in 37 3/4. On she sped, without a skip or break. . . . Then she began to go faster, and reached the three-quarter pole in 1:50 1/2. Everybody who had a watch had it out and was anxiously watching the filly. On she came, as steady as clockwork. The pacer began to draw up on her and she trotted faster every moment. When she passed under the wire the watches said 2:27 1/4, and the track was instantly filled with a shouting crowd of enthusiasts who wanted to hug the little roan. This is the fastest mile ever trotted by a two-year-old outside of California. [Can you hear that, Kentuckians?] Truly a wonderful performance for a two-year-old. This closed the sport . . . Every member is enthusiastic over the meet and particularly so over Mamie Wood's performance.[113]

---

113 "Mamie Wood Breaks a Record", September 10, 1886, <u>fultonhistory.com</u>.

Mamie Wood was the darling of the week. She had bested the Kentucky colt's record time by a margin of 1 3/4 seconds! At least six newspapers carried versions of her achievement, however detailed or brief. Her big brother, Floodwood, however, did not share her success at Rochester that week. He had been distanced in his three-year-old stallion stakes race; he was out of the running for that go round. The Erie train took them home to Fassett. As the triumphant news reached the Kentucky breeders, the New York horsemen had their moment of pride, in themselves and in Mamie.

Thomas Flood was a Republican. Most of the prominent newspapers of the day were politically slanted and unapologetically rancorous. Grover Cleveland was in his first term at the White House, and big business rolled unhindered across the Manifest Destiny land. Under Cleveland almost everything ran roughshod. Tammany Hall corruption, racial separation, and bias against foreign immigrants went unquestioned. Indian shows featured "wild savages," as they were supposedly found on the western prairies, and temperance was the big social issue, not women's rights. Rights to what? The headlines beside the racing news shock one's current sensibilities. A Mexican marauder terrorized the Texas border. Train wrecks, mine explosions, factory fires, and tannery accidents filled headlines. Lumber mill labor unrest in Williamsport, Pennsylvania, quelled by fatal sprays of gunfire, revealed a very different era. Life was cheap among the working poor and immigrant underclass. Current perceptions of gender and race equity, politics, human and animal cruelty, social issues, and the like are stretched to the point of squirming discomfort when one reaches back into time to process the context of the late nineteenth century.

During the later months of 1886, Flood was very much occupied with politics. He was nominated to run for the US House as a representative from New York state's twenty-eighth district, which included the counties of Chemung, Steuben, and Yates. The area was heavily Democrat, and the long-standing incumbent, Hon. Jeremiah McGuire from Chemung, had been Speaker of the House. Flood's popularity propelled him along as it had in 1882 when he ran for local office. An energetic fellow, he was spreading himself quite thin campaigning in this election and following his passion for racehorses, all while continuing his pharmacist business in downtown Elmira.

Along with his many friends, he had critics—critics who claimed he could not possibly represent them well in Washington while dabbling so heavily in horses, and who claimed that his first love was playing, not working. As election day drew near, worried Democrats in Watkins (the Glen part of the name was added later) reprinted the following piece from the *Elmira Gazette*, a satire of theoretical conversation between Flood and a random congressional colleague, should he get to DC:

Scene at Washington (Re-printed from Elmira Gazette)

IF Tom Flood should be elected Congressman, how he would entertain his fellow representatives:

Congressman- "Mr. Flood, what is your opinion on the silver question?"

Flood- "I dunno. Say, have you got any good horses down here?"

C- "Yes, I am told there is some very fine stock here. What do you think—"

Flood- "Got any remarkable two-year-olds?"

C- "Well, I don't know as to that. What do you think—"

Flood- "I'll go a hundred there isn't one that can beat my Mamie Woods. Any good brood mares owned by any of the Senators?"

C- "I guess not, Mr. Flood. They hardly have time to look
after brood mares, but as I was saying what do you think—"
Flood- "Mary Ann is getting along well in years now. But
I tell you she has had some remarkable colts. Why I have
sold $10,000 worth of her get and still have a half
a dozen. I've got a yearling that can trot a half
in 1:50. How's that?"
C- "I should judge that was pretty fast for a colt, but,
as I was saying, what do you think—"
Flood- "I suppose there must be some good stallions kept
around here. Now I tell you I've a got a rattler and
he's made me some money. Oh, I've got a complete
stock farm, I—"
C- "Do you always carry it with you, sir?"
Flood- "Carry it with me? Oh, ah, that's good now.
No, oh, no. My colts are up at Elmira on the old
driving park. There are some fine ones I tell you.
There's Nellie Mayo. She's a darling, and there's— "
C- "Mr. Flood, are you a free-trader?"
Flood- "No, sir-ee I'm a hoss trader. To be sure I
generally sell all my colts for a cash consideration, but—"
But his auditor had fled.[114]

But he won the seat, shocking the Twenty-Eighth District
Democrats in November as he had shocked the Kentucky horsemen earlier that fall. He was so busy that he sent his cousin and
erstwhile reinsman, Frank Flood, to represent him at the New York
State Trotting Horse Breeders' Association meeting at Rochester in

---

114 *Watkins Democrat*, Scene at Washington, October 27, 1886, <u>fultonhistory.com</u>.

December shortly after the election. Flood pulled his weight within the association by sponsoring the Magnolia Farm Stakes race each September at the Breeders' meet, and Frank was on hand at the meeting to reup the support in Flood's absence. It was common for members to pitch money into a given stakes, which was then named for their farm, like trophy donors at today's livestock shows. Underwriting a prize was part of playing the game, which was separate from the pool selling and betting on the races in the big time.

Mamie's only other appearance that year was in Ravenna, Ohio, where Flood took her for a two-year-old class on September 22. This was a much slower group. She trotted only two heats against two other rivals, and won them both. They were slow heats, each over three minutes.[115]

After spending the winter at home in Fassett, Mamie Wood got an invitation to go to Kentucky for the summer of 1887. Mr. Ed Tipton, secretary of the Kentucky horse breeders' association "very cordially" invited Flood to bring Mamie down to the bluegrass to take part in their breeders' meet.[116] "Come a little closer," said the spider to the fly. "Let us see if your northern filly can hold her record against us down here on our home turf." Flood entered Mamie in a match race at home in Elmira for the Fourth of July, but she could not make 2:30 that day; she was three seconds too slow.

Mamie was entered in the New York stakes at Rochester for their meet at the end of August in the Village Farm Stakes. Underwritten by C. J. Hamlin, this stake was for foals born in 1884. Hamlin's stock were plentiful at these meets. Mamie's traveling companions from home this summer would be a younger half sister (a daughter of Mary Ann but not Old Dan) named Nellie Mayo and another

---

115 Wallace, *Year-Book*, vol. 2, 101.

116 *Cuba Patriot*, May 26, 1887, fultonhistory.com.

chestnut filly, Daisy Flood.[117] Also along for the Breeders' meet from Flood's farm were Mamie's older half-sister, Edith Almont (out of Mary Ann, not by Old Dan) and a roan gelding with no name who was purportedly sired by Old Dan.

When August 30 came, Mamie trotted in her designated class against two other stud colts, Cheltenham and Happy Gothard. Cheltenham won the first heat, Mamie came in second, and Happy Gothard was distanced. With only Mamie left to start against Cheltenham for the second heat, he left her behind and was awarded the class with times of 2:32 1/2 and 2:30. The next day, Mamie again started in a stakes race against only Happy Gothard. They trotted two heats, and Mamie won them both to take the class with faster times, 2:25 1/2 and 2:26 1/2. Was Charles Dunham driving Mamie? That same day, her stablemate, Mabel Flood, paced against the stopwatch.[118]

The very next week, September 8, found Mamie in Toledo, Ohio, where she won a stakes race for three-year-olds over one other mare. In St. Louis, Missouri, she trotted another stakes race for three-year-olds but ended up at the bottom of the batch, placing out of the money.

Boarding the horse railcar south, Mamie made her way to Kentucky to accept her invitation for that state's Trotting Horse Breeders' Association annual meeting on October 12. Flood had been specially requested to test her mettle against their best three-year-olds, with her record made the previous year on everyone's minds. With her loss in Missouri so fresh, did Flood doubt Mamie

---

117 *Spirit of the Times*, August 20, 1887, <u>fultonhistory.com</u>.
118 John Hankins Wallace, *Wallace's Year-Book of Trotting and Pacing in 1887*, vol. 3, Hathitrust Digital Library.

could measure up to the Kentucky colts she had been summoned to meet in Lexington?

> Mamie Wood is owned by the Hon. Thomas S. Flood of Elmira, and she is by Wood's Hambletonian out of Mary Ann, a celebrated broodmare by Magnolia. Her [Mamie's] three-year-old record is 2:27 1/4. She went to Lexington in October, the very heart of the colt-breeding and colt-maturing district, and although just recovering from a spell of sickness, she distanced, in a very stubborn contest, a field of three year olds, including Ben Hur, Lynnette and Princess Russell. . . . The Kentuckians were struck dumb with astonishment. They did not believe it possible for a Northern-bred three year old to come to Kentucky and there beat a packed field of Kentucky-bred colts . . .[119]

Mamie had done just that, and lowered her own best time as well, taking all three heats in 2:28, 2:26, and 2:27 1/2. The North-South rivalry was on. The northern papers gleefully embellished their accounts of the stake as they recounted Mamie Wood's victory down south.

The year of 1887 was another milestone for the Woods back in Deerfield as well. A new baby was born to Joseph and Myrtilla after a space of many years, a daughter, whom they named Edna.

After the demise of the local racecourse at Academy Corners, the horsemen of the Cowanesque Valley had no place to hold their own trotting events. The Cowanesque Valley Agricultural Society

---

119 *Buffalo Express*, August 5, 1888, <u>fultonhistory.com</u>.

formed in the mid-1880s. After raising funds for a couple of years, the society purchased land in Westfield and built a racetrack to be used in conjunction with their new fair. Everyone in the valley eagerly anticipated its first event, held in October of 1887:

> The new grounds are located on the Caleb Trowbridge farm about one mile above, or rather west of, Westfield. The Society recently purchased the whole farm of 112 acres for $5,000. Something over thirty acres have been appropriated for the Fair grounds, and substantial buildings have been erected at a cost of about $3,000 or $4,000, not counting the work which was contributed by members of the Society. On the broad flat is one of the finest trotting courses in this part of the State. It cost the Society $1,800. One side of the track runs along at the base of a bench of land which slopes gently down to the flat, and this "grand stand" formed by Nature herself will accommodate all the people that will be likely to want to see a horse race. Every inch of the track can be seen from any point of this beautiful slope.[120]

The new fair was a festive occasion, even though the early October weather was cloudy and chilly with a few snow flurries. The fair gathered in for exhibit the best of what the farms had produced. There was a Durham bull that weighed 2,600 pounds, and the draft horses on hand included a contingent of twenty-three Percherons brought by Henry Tubbs from his Riverside Stock Farm in Osceola.

---

120 *Wellsboro Agitator*, October 18, 1887, Green Free Library Newspaper Archives.

If chickens, pigs, or sheep were not your interest, a circus tent offered entertainment. There were categories for butter and cheese, and youngsters could enter a pet fox or raccoon for a prize!

As the year 1887 progressed into early 1888, Joseph Wood began construction on a new status symbol: a spacious new barn. The L-shaped expanse behind the new house had box stalls for the stud horses, room for the Woods' own teams and dairy cows, and more stalls for the breeding clientele—the visiting mares who might be boarding for a few weeks at a time. Gambrel roofs towered over two separate hay mows, with pulleys going each way to put away the required hay overhead. In those days before balers, hay was put away loose during the summer and only pressed in winter for sale or shipment on the railroad. Space-saving hay bales were not part of the farmer's life. Each wing of the barn had a large louvered cupola to keep the hay dry and give the animals ventilation. Forming a protective shield against the prevailing west wind down the valley, the slate roof bore the ultimate advertising hallmark: on the sides that faced the river road, the roof tiles spelled out the phrase "Jos. Wood 1888." The modest farmer was proud of his reputation as a horseman.

In April of 1888, Wood's Hambletonian died. He was a local legend, a celebrity of the horse community, and the Wood family's claim to fame. That he was beloved was proven by the good care given him over his lifetime by Oliver and then Joseph. He had lived a long life for a horse: thirty years. As the old stallion breathed his last, his first- and second-generation colts and fillies took off and began to fill the statistics books of the Standardbred registers and the newspaper headlines at the Grand Circuit races.

The summer of 1888 horse gossip picked up again as the track writers swarmed around the rails. Horace Brown, the trainer from Village Farm in East Aurora, was driving Hamlin's darling mare,

Belle Hamlin, and spectators watching the early morning training sessions at the race park were thrilled with her speed and gracefulness. Another of Hamlin's horses, Mocking Bird, was going to meet up with Mamie soon, and one columnist's speculation about the season's brightest four-year-olds went something like this:

> Mamie Woods has come to the front with an unexpected, astonishing rush. This is accounted for by the fact of Mamie Wood's [sic] having gone a mile in private at a very fast gait, which has just leaked out. Mamie is an Elmira horse, and her owner, T. S. [Flood], doesn't scare worth a cent at the size of the Kentucky boodle. He knows the pedigree of his horse and has every confidence in her sire, Wood's Hambletonian. To prove this he put up $1,000 today that Mamie could beat the winner's record. Hamlin's Mocking Bird has dropped a little in the books, perhaps through the disappointing of Justina[121] yesterday, but the Village Farm stable hasn't a fear but that the Bird will finish near the wire.[122]

Flood did not put Mamie in any Grand Circuit races the summer of 1888. Instead, he entered her in smaller venues and fairs, including exhibitions and show classes at the Buffalo International Fair. Held at the Buffalo Driving Park, the fair was an extravaganza with wide-ranging entertainments from displays of cut flowers to circuses

---

121 Justina was another of Hamlin's favorites and can be seen with Belle Hamlin in the engraving of the pole team driven by C. J. Hamlin. Hamlin campaigned them separately and as a team. Neither mare had a connection to Wood's Hambletonian, though Hamlin over the years had also purchased several broodmares from Joseph Wood.

122 *Buffalo Evening News*, Aug. 3, 1888, fultonhistory.com.

to "wild Indian" shows. There were type classes that resembled a beauty pageant in which the horses were led out at halter in front of the grandstand and lined up while the judges walked around them and compared their legs, feet, muscle tone, head shape, and pedigree with the others of their age all in a row. Mamie and three other fillies from Flood's trotting stables were judged on their various attributes according to age. Mamie won first place in her age group: mare, four years old and over. Her premium: $300. She was not a filly anymore; after her birthday she was considered a mare.[123]

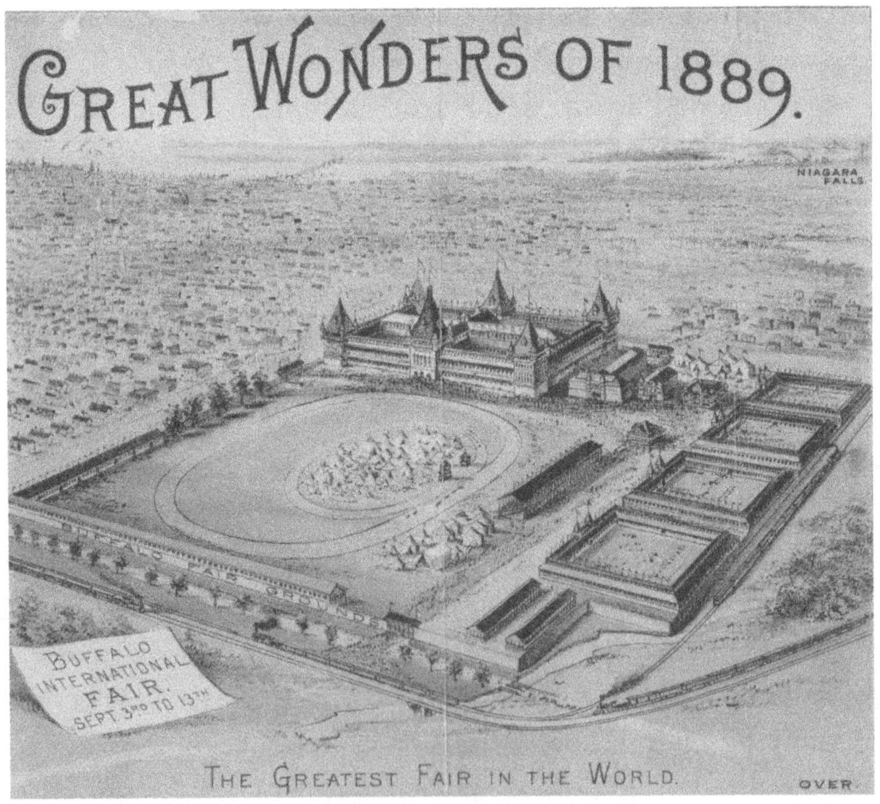

HAMLIN'S BUFFALO DRIVING PARK DURING THE DAYS OF THE BUFFALO INTERNATIONAL FAIR. (COURTESY BUFFALO HISTORY MUSEUM.)

---

123 *Buffalo Lightning Express*, September 7, 1888, <u>fultonhistory.com</u>

Mamie stayed at the fairgrounds to trot in her much-anticipated four-year-old stakes race against Hamlin's chestnut mare, Mocking Bird, who was a daughter of his acclaimed Mambrino King. On the tenth of September, she beat Mocking Bird and another mare named Gretna in three straight heats to win the class. Her new fastest heat was 2:25 1/4. For the first money in a purse that totaled $155, the bragging rights for Flood were more important than whether her share even paid her way there. The halter class was more lucrative that week.[124] Two days later at the same meet, Mamie's niece, Nightingale, won her three-year-old stake, a harbinger of things to come. Mamie's older brother, Floodwood, though, was still not panning out as Flood had hoped. The chestnut horse was distanced again in the 2:40 class and not performing up to expectations.

On September 26, Mamie trotted in Binghamton, New York, in the 2:24 class for a $400 purse. Her driver was Charles Dunham, and she won the second heat in 2:33 and the third heat in 2:27 to earn second money in that race. Mamie then went to the Duchess County Agricultural Society Fair held at Poughkeepsie, New York , on October 10. Mocking Bird, her rival from Village Farm, was also in that class, and this time Mocking Bird beat Mamie in all three heats. Nightingale was also at that fair, but she didn't go against Mamie because she was entered in the three-year-old classes for fillies.[125]

If things seemed quiet in Mamie's career that season, her driver, Charles Dunham, was about to liven things up. Thomas Flood was occupied, likely in Washington, and had entrusted Mamie's itinerary and care to Dunham for the previous several months. When she

---

124 John Hankins Wallace, *Wallace's Year-Book of Trotting and Pacing in 1888.*, vol. 4.
125 Ibid.

missed a race in Albany and failed to show up by train at her next gig, folks began to cable Flood with questions:

MAMIE WOODS ATTACHED: THE GREATEST TWO-YEAR-OLD HELD FOR A DEBT AT ALBANY

No little excitement was created among the horsemen of the city the past week, when the news was circulated that Congressman Flood's celebrated two-year-old,[126] Mamie Woods, had been seized at Albany for a debt. The queen of steppers had been entered for the meeting at Albany, but the races had been declared off on account of bad weather. The next meeting that she had been entered for was at Jersey City. When the races were called the animal failed to appear, and Mr. Flood was accordingly notified. About the same time he was also notified by William Miller, a stable keeper at Albany, that the animal was there and held for $75, which the driver of the animal, Charles Dunham, had borrowed. Henderson Gaylord, Esq., was immediately sent to Albany by Mr. Flood to investigate the cause of the mystery. Upon arriving there Mr. Gaylord found that Dunham had been on a spree, incurred the indebtedness claimed, and the animal was held as security. Dunham, he also learned, had been taken to Buffalo by an officer from that city, to straighten out an unsettled obligation of a large amount that he had

---

126 Though by 1888 she was four years old, the writer still made reference to her previous status.

contracted there some months ago. After considerable difficulty Mr. Gaylord arranged matters satisfactorily and returned yesterday to Elmira. The queen of the turf will follow and will soon be quartered at the congressman's stock farm at Gilletts, [sic] where she will remain until the opening of the spring circuit. She is valued at $8,000 by the congressman. She is at present in charge of the sheriff of Albany county, having been replevined by Mr. Gaylord from the stable keeper.[127]

Mamie was coming home for the winter, and she was likely going to get a new driver before she went on the railroad again. Thomas Flood had his hands full, finishing up his second term in Congress in Washington, DC, in 1888. With a wife and children based in Elmira, a horse farm in Fassett, a job in Washington, and racehorses traveling on the Grand Circuit, he delegated tasks to others. That always had its ups and downs.

Mamie's name recognition in the horse world was used for marketing in 1888, when Thomas S. Flood endorsed the brand Bege Remedies in a block advertisement, writing, "Magnolia Stock Farm—Dear Sir: I have used your Bege Blistering Ointment in my stable for the past ten years and consider it the best absorbent blister I have ever used. —Thos. S. Flood, owner Mamie Woods, 2 years, 2:27 1/4."[128] Said ointment could be purchased from George J. Burt, Pennsylvania Avenue, Elmira, New York.

On August 21, 1889 Mamie trotted in a stakes race for five-year-olds in Auburn, New York, and beat one other rival in three heats for first money, although she was slower, going 2:35 and 2:37 that day.

---

127   *Elmira Telegram*, November 4, 1888, <u>fultonhistory.com</u>.
128   *Spirit of the Times*, November 1888, <u>fultonhistory.com</u>.

During September, Mamie made halter-class appearances at some of the western New York county fairs. With several of her half siblings, she went to Hornellsville, Wellsville, Ithaca, and Elmira to greet fans and win premiums and ribbons.

She trotted in Milton, Pennsylvania, on October 4 but got third place there. From there she rode the train to Bloomsburg and on October 12 won first money in a $400 free-for-all stake, but with much slower times: 2:34 to 2:46. Her stablemate, the pacing mare Mabel Flood, was along for the trip as well.

Headed on to Philadelphia Driving Park for November 5, Mamie struggled in a big field, and placed well down in the 2:24 class. Darkness forced the final heats into the next day, the sixth. Mamie ended up with fourth money, but she was gaining experience as part of a larger pack. It seems that Thomas Flood's cousin, Frank Flood, who was also a doctor, was driving Mamie, and she stayed at that park and trotted again the next day, November 7. In a large field of eight, Mamie was going much faster that day and won the first two heats in 2:24 1/2 and 2:24 1/4, but the field was well matched and it stretched out to five heats with no winner when dusk settled in. The competition was stiff, and the next day Mamie won the final heat to garner her first money in the biggest, toughest batch of rivals she had come up against in her life. She went home to Magnolia Farm for the winter.

Was she ready for the big time, the Grand Circuit for 1890?

Mamie started off the summer season of 1890 in May, in Washington, DC, On May 2, she was in a field of three horses for the 2:20 class there. She broke gait several times in the first heat and struggled to follow the other two horses in both the first and second heats. She won the third and fourth heats but lost the last heat by two lengths.[129] Two weeks later Mamie was in Baltimore, Maryland, but she trotted dead last and was distanced, pulled out of the class. At the bottom of a four-horse field, she was clearly off her game.

It is not clear who started Mamie that season, but at some point that summer Flood put Mamie into the charge of a different trainer, a rising star on the Grand Circuit himself: William L. Snow. Snow was a native of Spring Mills, later known as Whitesville, in rural Allegany County. Snow's talent with horses was becoming widely known throughout the region and the Grand Circuit. In 1890 he was still based in Spring Mills. Snow took on up to two dozen horses at a time, and these horses belonged to many different owners, from close to home, like Flood, to Kentucky and Tennessee men as well. There were, however, several of Mamie's lesser-known kin on the Grand Circuit and other venues all summer that year: Maudie Belle, Jenny B., Bucephalus, Anna M., and of course the rising star, Mamie's niece from the Hamlins: Nightingale.

---

129 *New York Sun*, May 3, 1890, <u>fultonhistory.com</u>.

JULY 31, 1890.   THE AMERICAN SPORTSMAN.   75

1890 — THE — 1890
GRAND OLD CIRCUIT
PREMIUMS $230,000 PREMIUMS
The Annual Series of the World's Greatest Trotting Events!

PITTSBURGH	CLEVELAND,	BUFFALO,	ROCHESTER,	POUGHKEEPSIE,
JULY 22, 23, 24, 25.	JULY 29, 30, 31, AUG. 1.	AUG. 5, 6, 7, 8.	AUG. 12, 13, 14, 15.	AUG. 19, 20, 21, 22.

HARTFORD,	SPRINGFIELD	NEW YORK,	PHILADELPHIA,
AUG. 26, 27, 28, 29.	SEPT. 2, 3, 4, 5.	SEPT. 9, 10, 11, 12.	SEPT. 16, 17, 18, 19.

Pittsburg Driving Club.
$17,000.

TUESDAY, JULY 22.

2:30 class, trotting .... Purse $1,000
2:25 class, pacing .... Purse 1,000
2:20 class, trotting .... Purse 1,000

WEDNESDAY, JULY 23.

2:27 class, trotting .... Purse $1,000
Free-for-all class, pacing (Johnston barred) .... Purse 1,000

THURSDAY, JULY 24.

2:33 class, trotting .... Purse $1,000
2:17 class, pacing .... Purse 1,000
2:31 class, trotting .... Purse 1,000

FRIDAY, JULY 25.

2:23 class, trotting .... Purse $1,000
Free-for-all class, trotting (Guy barred) .... Purse 2,000
2:20 class, trotting .... Purse 1,000

$5,000 reserved for specials, to be announced hereafter.
Entries close Monday, July 7, 1890. Address
J. A. McCRACKEN, Secretary,
Post-office box 73, Pittsburg, Pa.

Cleveland Driving Park Co.
$30,500.

TUESDAY, JULY 29.

2:30 class, trotting .... Purse $2,000
2:25 class, pacing .... Purse 1,500
2:21 class, trotting .... Purse 2,000

WEDNESDAY, JULY 30.

2:27 class, trotting .... Purse $2,000
Free-for-all class, pacing (Johnston barred) .... Purse 1,500
2:19 class, trotting .... Purse 2,000

THURSDAY, JULY 31.

2:23 class, trotting .... Purse $3,000
Grand special (reserved) .... Purse 10,000
2:17 class, trotting .... Purse 2,000

FRIDAY, AUGUST 1.

2:22 class, trotting .... Purse $2,000
2:17 class, pacing .... Purse 1,500
Free-for-all class, trotting (Guy barred) .... Purse 2,000
Entries close Monday, July 21.
W. H. FASIG, Secretary.

Buffalo Park.
$32,000.

TUESDAY, AUGUST 5.

2:30 class, trotting .... Purse $2,000
2:21 class, pacing .... Purse 2,000
2:20 class, trotting .... Purse 2,000

WEDNESDAY, AUGUST 6.

2:27 class, trotting .... Purse $2,000
Free-for-all class, pacing (Johnston barred) .... Purse 2,000
2:19 class, trotting .... Purse 2,000

THURSDAY, AUGUST 7.

2:24 class, trotting .... Purse $2,000
Grand specials (reserved) .... Purse 10,000
Trotting, five-year-olds and under .... Purse 2,000

FRIDAY, AUGUST 8.

2:22 class, trotting .... Purse $2,000
2:17 class, pacing .... Purse 2,000
Free-for-all class, trotting (Guy barred) .... Purse 2,000

Entries to free-for-all trotting class and 2:17 pacing class close Saturday, August 2. All other classes closed. Second payment, 3 per cent, due July 1; third payment, 2½ per cent, due July 15 (at which time horses must be named); final payment, 2½ per cent, due August 2.
EDWARD S. HAWLEY, Secretary,
No. 7 Seneca St., W. Buffalo N. Y.

Rochester Driving Park.
$34,500.

TUESDAY, AUGUST 12.

Flower City Stake, 2:33 class, trotting (closed, with twenty nominations) $10,000
2:25 class, pacing .... Purse 1,500
2:21 class, trotting .... Purse 2,000

WEDNESDAY, AUGUST 13.

2:17 class, trotting .... Purse $2,000
Free-for-all class, pacing (Johnston barred) .... Purse 1,500
2:27 class, trotting .... Purse 2,000

THURSDAY, AUGUST 14.

2:17 class, trotting .... Purse $2,000
2:24 class, trotting, two-mile dash .... Purse 1,500
2:21 class, trotting .... Purse 2,000

FRIDAY, AUGUST 15.

Special .... Purse $3,000
2:25 class, trotting .... Purse 2,000
Free-for-all class, trotting (Guy barred) .... Purse 2,000
2:17 class, pacing .... Purse 1,500
Entries close Monday, July 21.   A. COLLINS, Secretary.

Hudson River Driving Park.
$12,500   Poughkeepsie, N. Y. $12,500

TUESDAY, AUGUST 19.

2:30 class, trotting .... Purse $1,000
2:25 class, pacing .... Purse 1,000

WEDNESDAY, AUGUST 20.

2:30 class, trotting .... Purse $1,500
2:27 class, trotting .... Purse 1,500
Free-for-all class, pacing (Johnston barred) .... Purse 1,000

THURSDAY, AUGUST 21.

2:18 class, trotting .... Purse $1,500
2:24 class, trotting .... Purse 1,500
Grand special, to be announced hereafter .... Purse 5,000

FRIDAY, AUGUST 22.

2:22 class, trotting .... Purse $1,500
Free-for-all class, trotting (Guy barred) .... Purse 1,500
2:17 class, pacing .... Purse 1,000
Entries close Monday, August 4.
D. B. HERRINGTON, Manager.

Charter Oak Driving Park.
$35,000.

TUESDAY, AUGUST 26.

2:30 trotting stake (closed) .... Purse $3,000
2:25 class, pacing .... Purse 2,000
2:21 class, trotting .... Purse 2,000

WEDNESDAY, AUGUST 27.

2:20 trotting stake (closed) $10,000
2:27 class, trotting .... Purse 1,500
2:23 class, trotting .... Purse 1,500

THURSDAY, AUGUST 28.

2:20 pacing stake (closed) $4,000
2:18 class, trotting .... Purse 2,000
2:25 class, trotting .... Purse 1,500

FRIDAY, AUGUST 29.

Four-year-old stake, trotting (closed) $5,000
Free-for-all class, trotting (Guy barred) .... Purse 7,000
Free-for-all class, pacing (Johnston barred) .... Purse 2,000
Three per cent, final payment on closed stakes due August 15, when horses must be named.
Entries to class races close Friday, August 15.
Address
T. O. KING, Secretary,
Hartford, Conn.

Hampden Park Association
$27,500   Springfield, Mass. $27,500

TUESDAY, SEPTEMBER 2.

2:30 class, trotting .... Purse $1,500
2:29 class, trotting .... Purse 1,500
Grand special, announced later .... Purse 2,000

WEDNESDAY, SEPTEMBER 3.

2:25 class, trotting .... Purse $1,500
2:22 class, trotting; Hampden Park stake (closed, eight subscribers) 5,000
Free-for-all class, pacing (Johnston barred) .... Purse 1,500

THURSDAY, SEPTEMBER 4.

2:18 class, trotting .... Purse $1,500
2:22 class, pacing; Massasoit Stake (closed, eight subscribers) 5,000
Grand special .... Purse 3,000

FRIDAY, SEPTEMBER 5.

2:24 class, trotting .... Purse $1,500
2:25 class, trotting; Springfield Stake (closed, eight subscribers) 5,000
2:17 class, pacing .... Purse 1,500
Entries to class races close Monday, August 18.
E. C. ROBINSON, Secretary and Treasurer,
Springfield, Mass.

New York Driving Club.
$16,500.

TUESDAY, SEPTEMBER 9.

2:37 class, trotting .... Purse $1,000
2:24 class, pacing .... Purse 1,000
2:34 class, trotting .... Purse 1,000

WEDNESDAY, SEPTEMBER 10.

2:37 class, trotting .... Purse $1,000
2:29 class, trotting .... Purse 1,500

THURSDAY, SEPTEMBER 11.

2:30 class, trotting .... Purse $1,000
Grand special (reserved) .... Purse 5,000
2:18 class, trotting .... Purse 1,000

FRIDAY, SEPTEMBER 12.

2:22 class, trotting .... Purse $1,000
2:22 class, trotting .... Purse 1,500
Free-for-all class, pacing (Johnston barred) .... Purse 1,000
Entries close Monday, August 25. Address
The Driving Club of New York, Morrisania, N. Y.
Augustus Raymond, Secretary.

Philadelphia Driving Park Association.

Programme to be Announced Later.

CONDITIONS—National Trotting Association Rules: All races in harness, best three in five, unless otherwise specified. Customary division of moneys, 50 per cent, 25 per cent, 15 per cent, and 10 per cent. Entrance fee 10 per cent. Right reserved to change the order of any day's programme. Right reserved to reject any entry of which notice is not received within twenty-four hours after hour of closing. Usual weather clause conditions.

F. L. Noble, George Rubens and C. H. Nelson, together with the horses Alcryon and Nelson, are barred from any participation on the tracks of the Grand Circuit in 1890. This condition is adopted as an endorsement of the action of the last Congress of the National Trotting Association.

All horses on the grounds will be charged 50 cents per day for keep.

REMEMBER THAT ENTRIES CLOSE AS FOLLOWS:

Pittsburg Driving Park, Monday, July 7, 1890. Address J. A. McCracken, Sec'y, P. O. Box 73, Pittsburg, Pa.
Cleveland Driving Park Company, Monday, July 21, 1890. Address William B. Fasig, Sec'y, Cleveland, Ohio.
Buffalo Entries for Free-for-All Close Friday, Aug. 1, 1890. Address Edward S. Hawley, Sec'y, 7 Seneca-st., Buffalo.
Rochester Driving Park, Monday, July 21, 1890. Address W. Collins, Sec'y, Rochester, N. Y.
Hudson River Driving Park, Monday, August 4, 1890. Address D B. Herrington, Man'g'r, Houghkeepsie, N.Y.

SCHEDULE OF GRAND CIRCUIT FOR 1890, *THE AMERICAN SPORTSMAN*, JULY 31, 1890. MAMIE WOOD AND NIGHTINGALE BOTH CAMPAIGNED THIS SUMMER.

Mamie's times and performance were up and down that summer, but she was booked for a constant traveling schedule, and she was holding her own. She didn't do well on July 8 in Philadelphia, dropping out of the last heat in a field of thirteen that had extended a brutal eight heats into the next day. Nor did she shine on July 16 in Philadelphia, but she did manage to hold onto fourth money in a faster class. In Pittsburg[130] on July 25, she won first money in a $1,000 purse, taking three heats out of five. The next week she went to Cleveland, Ohio, but trotted near the bottom of the pack and dropped out of the class.

In Rochester, New York, for the middle of August, she was a bit out of her element but earned fourth money there. Even Nightingale, her hotshot niece, was pulled out of a $10,000 stakes race in Rochester that week. The Grand Circuit was rigorous traveling for the horses, and the next week, on August 21, Mamie and Nightingale were both in Poughkeepsie, New York, at the Hudson River Driving Park. There Mamie was trotting in eighth place out of nine horses, and she seemed tired, dropping out after the fourth heat. It was at Poughkeepsie that C. J. Hamlin made his stunning exhibition, driving his sought-after record with his favorite team of mares, Justina and Belle Hamlin, per the news archive illustration on the cover of *Clark's Horse Review*[131]. Some writers had called Mamie Wood "Queen of the Turf" and other gushing titles as a youngster, but it was hard to keep up expectations with such keen competition to be the darling of the press. Mamie seemed to have Hamlin's mares just one step ahead in the popularity polls.

---

130   Spelled with no *h* at the time.

131   The weekly journal *Clark's Horse Review* was published in Chicago, Illinois, from 1885 to the early 1890s, when its named was changed to *The Horse Review,* by which name it continued until 1932, mi-harness.net

C. J. Hamlin, foremost harness breeder of the era, who owned several horses from the Woods, including Nightingale. Cover of *Clark's Horse Review*, November 1, 1890.

There was no rest for Mamie; for her it was on to Charter Oak Park, in Hartford, Connecticut, for the end of August. Her old competitor, Mocking Bird, had moved up to a faster class, but Mamie stayed in the 2:25 slot and found her niche: she won all three heats and in faster times, too: 2:21, 2:21 3/4, and 2:20 1/2. The purse was $1,500 that day, and the last heat would stand as the fastest race of Mamie's career on the Grand Circuit—her record would stay at 2:20 1/2 for the books. Nightingale had gone to Hartford also; she would trot the following day. Mamie did not go against Nightingale, even though they followed the same route through the Grand Circuit that summer.

The following article sums up the events at the Charter Oak race meet:

The Grand Circuit followers understand the qualities and ability of the campaigners by the time Charter Oak Park is reached at Hartford, and there are few surprises during the week. Charter Oak Park was in good condition . . . and the time was fast considering that the horses that have fought race after race since early spring are in poor shape and rather stale . . .

On Thursday the famous Charter Oak $10,000 stake was decided, and for the fourth time was won by a stallion . . . Mamie Woods, who was a fast two-year-old, won her first Grand Circuit race, reducing her record to 2:20 1/2 at the same time . . . The important event on Saturday was the exhibition mile made by C. J. Hamlin, who drove a double team in 2:15 3/4... The performance of Belle Hamlin and Justina is the most remarkable when it is known that Mr. Hamlin bred, raised, and drove the team to this record, and no other man has yet driven a team of his own breeding in 2:40. Mr. Hamlin will make another attempt at Springfield this week.[132]

In the Buffalo papers, it was always going to be about Hamlin. The fifth of September found Mamie in Springfield, Massachusetts, at Hampden Park. Here Mamie and Nightingale also stabled together and likely jogged past each other on their way to warm up, each mare with her own driver, her own high-wheeled sulky, and her own job to do, unaware of the other's origins. Two

---

132   *Buffalo Courier*, September 1, 1890, <u>fultonhistory.com</u>.

of Old Dan's star mares overlapped on the Grand Old Circuit one golden summer. That summer ushered in the decade of the "Gay 90s"—a decade when technology would bring bicycle pneumatic tires to sulky racing and shave seconds off all records. It was to be a decade when harness racing enjoyed its zenith as an American spectator sport, before the motorcar, before the century turned, and before the Great War changed American life yet again.

Two days of heavy rains had postponed the race schedule and thinned the crowd, but Mamie did well at Springfield. She trundled through pouring rains on a muddy track to win all three heats, first money of a $1,500 purse.[133] If she was not the biggest star, she certainly deserved credit for being a durable competitor. The bad weather continued to plague the circuit, and five days later, on September 10 in New York City, the weather was lousy at the Fleetwood Park. A cold wind cut through people and horses as Mamie took on four rivals in the 2:24 class. She struggled but held her own at 2:24, no faster, no slower.

The news writer had this to say of her race: "Mamie Woods is also able to give the black gelding [Frank T.] a race, but her race at Springfield on Monday had left her sore. Before the last heat the judges took out Snow, who was driving the mare, and put [Millard] Sanders in his sulky. It might have had a better effect had they shifted some of the others."[134] Clearly the columnist thought something was amiss. Thomas Flood was on hand to watch the mare that day and claimed she was sore from trotting in the mud at Springfield.

Mamie may have been showing her limits of endurance when she had to drop out of two races in Philadelphia later in September. Meanwhile, Nightingale seemed to be picking up speed, winning in

---

133 *New York Herald*, September 7, 1890, fultonhistory.com.
134 *The World*, September 11, 1890, fultonhistory.com.

ever faster classes, while C. J. Hamlin kept doing his exhibition team display with Belle Hamlin and Justina as a sideline feature. Their new time was an astonishing 2:15 1/2. That season's Grand Circuit was over, but Mamie was not home yet. On October 1, she was at the smaller venue of Milton, Pennsylvania, and dropped out there. From there she was on the train to York, Pennsylvania, where she stayed in the class and held onto third place.

When spring came in 1891, Mamie was getting daily workouts at the Maple Avenue Driving Park on Elmira's south side in preparation for the upcoming summer season. Flood entered Mamie at Albany, but nowhere is she mentioned in any Grand Circuit races. Was she not up for it? Did she have an injury or illness? The *Elmira Telegram* reported in May:

> The Maple Avenue Driving Park presents a busy scene these fine spring mornings. There are about forty horses in training at the park stables, and within easy distance of the track, and most of them take their exercise there every day. There are always a number of interested spectators present. Owners and trainers are sure to be on hand . . . The event of the morning, yesterday, however, was the appearance of ex-Congressman Tom Flood behind his pacing mare Mabel, in a mile effort against his own Mamie Woods, the latter driven by Doc Moore. It had been hoped that the mares would have been in condition to make a good showing, but Mamie was not inclined to attend strictly to business, the pacer kept down to work in good shape, but Mamie was a long while in settling down, and the mile that she finally made was not better than

2:34 3/4. It will be remembered that she has a record of 2:20 [3/4] [sic], while the pacer is credited with 2:30.[135]

Mamie was scheduled for a busy summer that year, but she was entered in mostly regional venues, not the Grand Circuit. Whether she could not settle down and improve her times or whether Thomas Flood had tired of the Grand Circuit isn't clear (did the crackdown on betting in New York state occur that season and cause a downturn in track attendance and finances that led to the demise of the Circuit?), but her traveling itinerary was different.

She started at Belmont Park in Philadelphia on June 30, taking second money in the 2:20 class, but she could not earn top spots consistently after that. She started at Philadelphia Driving Park on July 7, went to Albany, New York, for July 16, and Syracuse, New York, on July 24, ending up out of the money standings. Mamie struggled to get her time below 2:30 in any of these starts, and though she won three out of five heats in Bradford, Pennsylvania, on August 28, she got second and third money, respectively, at her starts in Franklinville, New York, on September 18 and Cuba, New York, on September 25.

It was during that year that Flood set his sights on another high-level job: governor of New York state. He was going to make a bid for the Republican nomination at the convention to be held in Rochester, where the party would select its candidate for the May 1892 election. Among his financial backers were the wealthy Charles J. Langdon, brother-in-law of Mark Twain, and J. D. F. Slee, business partner of Twain's father-in-law, Jervis Langdon. Thomas Flood had moved in

---

135 "Among Fast Trotters," May 31, 1891, <u>fultonhistory.com</u>.

the power circles of Elmira his whole life, and as Elmira was a small city, everyone knew everyone else in the area.

Thomas K. Beecher, the iconic abolitionist preacher of the Park Church, was well-known as the brother of Harriet Beecher Stowe, whose novel *Uncle Tom's Cabin* had given voice to the abolitionist cause leading up to the Civil War. That Beecher had performed the wedding ceremony for Thomas Flood's sister at their elegant family home just a short time before he married Mark Twain to Olivia Langdon at her family's Italianate mansion a couple of blocks away in the same city was evidence of the connectedness of these people during the era.

Mark Twain cranked out much of *The Adventures of Huckleberry Finn* and some of his other best work in his cozy study on the hilltop overlooking the city while Thomas Flood raced horses at the fairground track below. The two men were starkly different. Twain's favorite fodder was to poke fun at politicians, and he preferred cats over horses. Flood juggled so many details it was doubtful he took time to ruminate deeply over any one topic. Did they ever shoot billiards together at the social hall? While no evidence was found that placed the two men side by side at the same event, they certainly shared mutual friends and the same neighborhood. Elmira was not that large.

So it was that in September of 1891, Flood assembled his political pals for the Republican convention, looking hopefully toward the nomination in Rochester. But he had a rival for the job, and that rival was equally well connected and well-heeled: Jacob Sloat Fassett. Fassett was a banker with diverse, lucrative mining and lumber interests and a solid political camp of his own. Many delegates throughout the region had not revealed their allegiance as the convention week arrived.

Thomas Flood had his own elegant Pullman sleeper car on the Erie rail line, and it was named in honor of his best racehorse, Mamie Wood. It was no horsecar; it was for transporting rich people in style and comfort, stocked with the best cigars and brandy money could buy. Boarding it for the trip to Rochester was a large delegation of men, including Charles Langdon and J. D. F. Slee. The outside of the Pullman was decorated with campaign banners. There was afoot, however, a coup among the voting delegates headed to Rochester. The sweeping, sudden change of support was rumored to be going Fassett's way, even as the railcars wound their way north to Rochester. The newspapers called it a "boom,"[136] a last-minute swing in Fassett's favor. After rancorous debate at the convention, Thomas Flood's group returned to Elmira the following day when Fassett's victory as the Republican candidate became clear.[137]

It was not the proudest day in Thomas Flood's career, but as politics required, he had diverse talents, plenty of friends, and a resilient personality. J. Sloat Fassett would not win the governorship, either, but he also went on to become a stronghold in regional and national politics, heading the Republican National Committee more than once. His fortune was perhaps most visible in the years to follow in the image of his extravagant West Elmira estate, the Strathmont, which had no peer in the region for size and scale.[138]

In early October, Mamie Wood trotted an exhibition at Meadville, Pennsylvania; then Flood shipped her down to Lexington, Kentucky,

---

136 "At Rochester", *Elmira Daily Gazette & Free Press,* September 9, 1891, <u>fultonhistory.com</u>

137 "A Modern King of Spain", *Elmira Telegram*, September 18, 1891, <u>fultonhistory.com</u>.

138 Alfred E. Edgcomb (1867–1933) brother of Waldo H. Edgcomb of Knoxville, Pennsylvania, became a partner with J. Sloat Fassett in a Canadian timber business and a mahogany-export lumber venture based in the Philippines. Alfred Edgcomb lived for many years in Germantown, near Philadelphia. (*Wellsboro Gazette*, April 27, 1933).

once more for the Kentucky Horse Breeders Association meeting there. But it was not Mamie's year to star in Kentucky: in a field of six other horses trotting the 2:21 class, she was pulled out of the first heat. There is no mention of details, whether she was exhausted or had an injury; she was just finished for that season. She had won only one race of the nine starts she made that summer.

In late winter, Thomas Flood put Mamie Wood and her pacing stable mate, Mabel Flood, into a consignment sale to be held out of Cleveland, Ohio. With them he consigned a couple of his brood-mares and a team of matched driving horses. Flood was downsizing his horse hobby, and Mamie's early fame as a filly had not translated into stardom as a mare. Lest Mamie take it personally, he was divesting himself of Mabel Flood, who had done very well that year.

Times were changing, and Flood once again had other irons in the fire. Always on the cutting edge of new capital ventures, his mind was captivated by the next trend: the gas and oil fields of Tioga and Potter Counties in Pennsylvania.[139] Although he kept Magnolia Farm, he dropped out of notice at the Chemung racing venues like Elmira Driving Park and Maple Avenue Park, places he had regularly appeared during his heady horse days. Flood's attention was being drawn elsewhere.

Always a venture capitalist, he formed with a group of friends and fellow investors the Elmira and Gaines Oil & Gas Company, whose goal was to explore and drill wells in Potter and Tioga Counties. They had reason to believe there were resources down there for the taking, in the lands owned by Billings in Gaines, in Tioga and Elkland, and in Pike and West Branch townships in Potter County.

---

139 *Elmira Telegram*, "Producers Spurred On," July 14, 1895, <u>fultonhistory.com</u>.

In 1895, he kicked in for a major share and installed himself as the director.[140]

He consigned ten more of his trotting horses in a New York sale as he moved into gas speculation. He continued to employ a manager to take care of the animals and the place in Fassett. He was listed among other businesses in Fassett in South Creek Township as "the Hotel in 1900 owned by Thomas Flood; Magnolia Stock Farm for raising horses" and was still entered on the real estate tax rolls for the township at that time.[141]

In the fall of 1900, he took the railroad west to Gaines, Pennsylvania, part of the Billings timber tracts, to check on his new project. The Gaines correspondent for the *Wellsboro Agitator* sent in the following news for the week of October 23: "Hon. T. S. Flood, of Elmira, N.Y., was in town last week. He still holds his oil interests here . . . The New York and Pennsylvania Oil and Gas Company are drilling a well on lot 3, Billings. If successful, they will develop the lease, which consists of 100 acres."[142] Did he catch the Buffalo & Susquehanna line west up through the Cowanesque Valley through the back fields of his old friend Joseph Wood? Would he have kept his nose in his newspaper as he trundled along or gazed out the windows at the horses and cows grazing there along the railroad?

Then in April of 1906, the barns at Magnolia Farm caught fire. The livestock, numbering ten horses and fifteen cows, were saved, but the big barn and the shed with farm implements and wagons were lost. The fire briefly spread to the church near the barn, but the church was saved.[143]

---

140 *Elmira Telegram*, July 14, 1895.

141 Henry G. Farley and Doris W. Hugo, *Bradford County History, 1891-1995* (Curtis Media, 1996).

142 October 1879, Green Free Library Newspaper Archives.

143 *Elmira Gazette & Free Press*, April 30, 1906, <u>fultonhistory.com</u>.

He had been referred to with the titles of "Honorable" and even "Commodore," as his political career and popularity followed him into his later years in business. He went to Pittsburg, Pennsylvania—at that time spelled with no *h*—to take care of some gas company business in the fall of 1908, caught pneumonia, and died there a few days later. His brother, Dr. Henry Flood, had traveled out when he got word of his brother's illness and was with him when he died. Flood was sixty-four.[144] Henry brought his brother home to Elmira for a family funeral and burial with other relatives in Woodlawn Cemetery. Flood's wife and son had previously died, and he was survived by his daughter, Dr. Frances Mabel Flood, later Heath. The extended family of Floods held a prominent place in medicine and politics in the city of Elmira. Thomas Flood's forays into lumber, railroads, and gas wells—and his passion for horses—secured his page in history as well.[145]

Meanwhile, back in March 1892, various newspapers published the news of Mamie's sale: "The Horseheads reporter says Hon. Thomas Flood's famous roan mare Mamie Woods,[sic] which has a record of 2:27 1/2 as a two-year-old, has been sold to a Kentucky breeder, for $1,830."[146]

The Kentucky breeder was William H. Wilson, the renowned horseman who had introduced the bloodline of the stallion George Wilkes to that state in 1873. The Wilkes line's biggest descendant

---

144 "Thomas S. Flood Dead," *Bolivar Breeze*, November 5, 1908, <u>fultonhistory.com</u>.

145 Ausburn Towner, *History of Chemung County, New York* (Syracuse, NY: D. Mason, 1892, repub. 1986), 676.

146 *The Ovid(NY) Independent*, March 15, 1892, <u>fultonhistory.com</u>.

was to become a household name at the turn of the century: the pacer Dan Patch. Dan Patch's story was well-chronicled in Leerhsen's *Crazy Good*. Wilson's extensive stables in Cynthiana were the hallmark of Standardbred breeding in Kentucky.

Mamie Wood may have stayed in Kentucky after her last race in October of 1891; her sale details are not clear. Had Wilson offered to buy her at the Lexington breeders' meet? That Wilson had long been aware of the Wood horses' track performance over the previous years is certain. He had campaigned trotters up in Erie, Pennsylvania, back in 1875 when his horses competed against horses put on the track by O. H. Wood during that season.[147]

At Wilson's stables in Cynthiana, Mamie was moving on to her next career. She was bred to the farm's well-known stud, Simmons #2744 (also a son of George Wilkes), shortly after her arrival. But Wilson himself was an aged fellow, and he died shortly thereafter, leaving a large operation in the hands of his heirs and executors.

Wilson's heirs may have been dispersing the stable during that year, however, because Mamie soon found herself traveling to a new home. She had a track career behind her, a solid trotting pedigree stretching back to Magnolia #68 and Wood's Hambletonian #572, and she was now in foal to another reputable stallion.[148]

Her new owner was not just any southern businessman; he was R. J. Reynolds, tobacco capitalist with a fortune that multiplied each year. Reynolds was acquiring tobacco and tobacco-processing plants around Lexington during that time, securing his holdings throughout the South. A lover of fine horses and with the money to pursue the sport almost without limits, like C. J. Hamlin, Thomas Flood,

---

147 *Buffalo Express*, July 15, 1875, <u>fultonhistory.com</u>.
148 *The Southern Planter*, vol. 64 (October 1903), 634, Hathitrust Digital Library.

Frank Work, and the Vanderbilts, Reynolds shipped Mamie Wood to his home in Winston, North Carolina.

At her new home in 1893, Mamie gave birth to her first foal, a brown filly, who was to be named Skyland Girl. Skyland Girl was trained in the pacing gait, having acquired this ability from her sire Simmons's Wilkes lineage. She started her track career driven by George Dyer.

Whether R. J. Reynolds had sold her is unclear, but by 1900 she appeared in a news column: "Well-known trainer and driver George F. Dyer, has moved to Winston, NC & assumed charge of the Piedmont Fair Assoc.'s grounds and track, where he is wintering a stable of trotters and pacers. . . . His stable now includes Skyland Girl, 2:28 pacing, by Simmons, 2:20, dam the well-known roan mare Mamie Woods,[sic] 2:20 [sic: 2:20 1/2] by Wood's Hambletonian."[149]

Mamie Wood dropped out of sight around 1903, after she was mentioned in another *Southern Planter* article about Skyland Girl. When R. J. Reynolds sold Mamie Wood and her first daughter Skyland Girl is unclear, but they were not part of his stable when he dispersed the remainder of his horses. R. J. Reynolds was another of those Gilded Age figures whose position in agriculture and industry shaped American culture, as had Hamlin's sugar fortune and Flood's lumber and railroad ventures. The Reynolds family's story is one of excessive wealth that descended into decadence and tragedy along yet a separate tangent.[150]

In an article summarizing the accomplishments of Skyland Girl published in *The Southern Planter*, the story of Mamie concluded as she faded into obscurity as a broodmare: "She [Skyland Girl] was

---

149 *The Southern Planter*, vol. 61 (February 1900), 95, Hathitrust Digital Library.
150 Tom Schachtman and Patrick Reynolds, *The Gilded Leaf:Triumph, Tragedy and Tobacco, (Lincoln, NE: BackinPrint by iUniverse.com, 1989)*.

sired by Simmons, a great son of George Wilkes, dam the once famous trotting mare, Mamie Woods,[sic] 2:20 1/2, by Wood's Hambletonian. Mamie Woods [sic]was purchased in Kentucky by Mr. Reynolds while carrying Skyland Girl in utero and after the latter was dropped the roan mare was bred to Baronet, 2:11 1/4, and other sires of more or less note."[151]

Skyland Girl campaigned on the harness circuit for several seasons under the guidance of Dyer and made her record in the summer of 1903. That season she started in ten races, beginning in June in Philadelphia, heading to New Paltz, New York, in August 12, then on to Liberty, New York, on August 21, where she won first money in the 2:19 class in a big field of ten pacers after a rough start.

She was lowering her times each week, and in Goshen, New York, in the historic village where old William Rysdyk had trotted his foundation sire, Hambletonian #10, so many decades earlier, Skyland Girl won first money of a $500 purse in the 2:20 class over heats that took two days, the twenty-sixth and twenty-seventh of August, to finish. Her personal-best mile time—2:14 1/2—she earned on September 2 at Poughkeepsie, New York, winning first money against six rivals. That time would stand as her fastest record. She went from there on to Orangeburg, New York, then Ridgewood, New York, and Allentown, Pennsylvania, where she ranged in the middle of her classes. She finished her season in Trenton, New Jersey, at the beginning of October, completing her classes but without a win.

Two noteworthy news items from the 1904 race circuit show the enduring nature of Skyland Girl's track performance. She was a mature mare of eleven years by this time, and she won a free-for-all pace

---

151 *The Southern Planter*, vol. 64 (October 1903), 634, Hathitrust Digital Library.

class at Weeguahic Park in Waverly, New Jersey, on July 17.[152] But she proved a few weeks later that she knew how to make it through a race, even without a driver! On August 6, she was entered in a large field of horses at Hudson River Park in Poughkeepsie, New York, when things went haywire:

> A driverless horse, Skyland Girl, trotted under the wire and won third money in the third heat of the 2:14 pacing race, while the driver was lying at the side of the track and being cared for by a physician. Skyland Girl, an intelligent brown mare, had second position in this heat, and at the first turn, after getting the word, one of the other drivers collided with her sulky. Driver Isaac Hully was thrown out, but escaped being killed as he lay on the track while the trotters swirled past. He was carried to the side of the track, and the sulky having righted itself, Skyland Girl, taking the outside position, made a strong effort to keep up with the bunch. She succeeded in getting sixth place, and was awarded third money. Hully was only brushed, as the wheel ran over his back. He was able to limp to the judge's stand, where he and his mare were applauded by the large attendance . . .[153]

Hully was no doubt grateful for her presence of mind and years of track experience. Exaggeration notwithstanding, the little story

---

152 "Matinee Trots at Weeguahic Park", *New York Herald*, July 17, 1904, <u>fultonhistory.com</u>.

153 "Driverless Horse in the Money", *New York Sunday Telegraph*, August 7, 1904, <u>fultonhistory.com</u>.

painted a colorful picture of something right out of an episode of *Lassie.* Whether it was around the racetrack or out on country roads doing errands, things always looked bad when the horse arrived home with the wagon seat empty.

Skyland Girl's final appearance in the news was when, as a thirteen-year-old road mare, she went through the winter consignment sale of racing stock Fasig-Tipton held in Madison Square Garden.[154]

And so concluded the legacy of Mamie Wood, a daughter of Old Dan from the northern breeding tradition whose sale to Kentucky joined her bloodline with that of the Wilkeses' to continue on the harness tracks as the twentieth century began. The relationship between Joseph Wood and Thomas Flood was a business connection spanning two decades. Joseph Wood sold broodmares and young stock to Flood's racing stable, and mares came from Elmira and Fassett to Deerfield over the dirt roads in the 1870s and the railways in the 1880s to be bred to the Woods' noteworthy stallion. Flood knew it was worth the trip. Thomas Flood's wide circle of travel and political connections presented a sharp contrast to the obscure location where the Woods on their Deerfield farm bred horses, milked cows, raised tobacco, and made hay. But it paralleled in time the burgeoning of the nation and showed the immense personal wealth that some capitalists amassed during the era named by Mark Twain himself: the Gilded Age.

---

154 *New York Times,* February 6, 1906, www.nytimes.com.

CHAPTER 6

NIGHTINGALE: GOING THE DISTANCE

C. J. (Cicero Jabez) Hamlin (1819–1905) was a leading figure in the harness-horse world. Hamlin had set about years before to breed the fastest and most handsome horses that money could produce. A self-made man in the early years of the Industrial Age, Hamlin amassed his wealth in retail and sugar production and had the cash to follow his fancy into harness racing, the most popular spectator sport of the era.

He first built barns in 1855 in the village of East Aurora, New York, near Buffalo. Best known as home of Elbert Hubbard's Roycroft movement, the village was first a mecca for horsemen. Hamlin called his place Village Farm and began to acquire horses. Most peripheral pastimes paused during the Civil War. But when it was over, Hamlin began to pursue his dream in earnest. By 1868, on the east side of Buffalo, he opened an oval, mile-long track to serve as both harness racing and polo grounds. In time it became known as the Buffalo Driving Park and later earned the nickname the Kentucky Derby of the North by drawing grandstand crowds of up to forty thousand people on weekends.[155] Hamlin's goal was to produce horses that were both speedy and pretty. He was once quoted as saying he liked to dance with pretty women and drive pretty horses. Up to that time some of the best road horses were not pleasant to behold, with coarse roman noses and ewe-necks commonly found. To that end, Hamlin went shopping around the nation.

After his visit to Joseph Wood in 1881, Hamlin continued his quest for the stud horse of his dreams, and he went to Kentucky and bought Mambrino King #1249 the following year. Mambrino King was ten years old, and some sources claimed the price Hamlin paid was as high as $25,000. A product of the prestigious Wilkes bloodline of horses, he became not only the backbone of Hamlin's breeding program but a tourist attraction as well. Grooms led him out of his barn often to be admired by his many fans who visited Village Farm. With the addition of another stud horse, Chimes #5348, Hamlin proceeded through the 1880s to breed the best to the best: the daughters of one stud directly to the other.[156]

At her new home in East Aurora, Minnequa Maid was bred to Mambrino King and foaled Nightingale on April 20, 1885. You could say that the chestnut filly was born with a "silver bit" in her mouth, the daughter of a stallion who was lauded as the most beautiful horse in the world. Minnequa Maid became a key broodmare at Village Farm, mothering a succession of foals for Hamlin. In the years after Nightingale, she produced Milan Chimes, Chimes Girl, Hereward, and the bad-boy gem Scapegoat. Other foals coming out

---

155 Mark Puma, "The History of Hamlin Park Part IV:
Hamlin's Driving Park and the Home Builders," *Buffalo Rising*,
August 21, 2013, https://www.buffalorising.com/2013/08/
the-history-of-hamlin-park-part-iv-hamlins-driving-park-and-the-home-builders/.
156 E. F. Geers, *Ed. Geers' Experience with the Trotters and Pacers* (Buffalo, NY: Matthews-Northrup, 1901), 78.

of Hamlin's breeding program were the stars of the decade: Lady of the Manor, The Monk, The Abbott, Belle Hamlin, Justina, Globe, and many others.

Hamlin's Village Farm, situated on the outskirts of the village of East Aurora, was without equal in the nation for its sheer size and singleness of purpose: to produce and race the fastest harness horses in the largest numbers. Hamlin's son, Harry Hamlin, joined him in the management of the large and varied livestock raised at the Village Farm, and both were involved in the decisions regarding harness horses. Harry Hamlin's great-grandson and namesake, actor Harry Hamlin, found fame during the 1990s on the sultry California TV drama series *LA Law*. During its peak years from about 1882 until the turn of the century, the farm was at times home to six hundred horses. In addition to light harness horses, the Hamlins raised heavy coach horses and purebred dairy cattle. They employed at least fifty men during the winters and more in the summer training and racing seasons. A virtual self-sufficient village made up of many buildings, the farm boasted one main barn for mares and young stock, another for stallions, another just for teams, a separate blacksmith shop, a veterinarian's barn, several employee residences, and two training tracks on the premises.

Nothing escaped C. J. Hamlin's attention, and he was particular about the atmosphere in his barns as well. Together with his long-time trainer, Ed Geers, he expected the horse barns to be quiet and genteel: "loud talk, profanity, vulgarity and obscenity have no proper place in a training stable. I have never known a horse to be benefited by any of these disgusting habits. The training stable should be conducted with the same degree of propriety that is observed in the transaction of any other legitimate business, and should at all times be a place where ladies, as well as all others, can visit without their sensibilities being shocked by hearing and seeing things to which their ears and eyes are not accustomed."[157]

What one might hear at the racetrack was anyone's guess, but ears were safe at Village Farm.

Hamlin published an annual catalog that included all the stock present at the farm. It listed the priciest senior stud horses with their breeding fees and the current campaigners with their best track times, and included the weanling colts or mares that might be for sale in a given year, with pedigrees. Most of the horses were owned by the Hamlins, but sometimes as many as two hundred horses owned by others were stabled there for breeding or race training.[158] Hamlin had his own horse railcar fitted out with stalls to transport his racing string on their extensive spring and summer schedules. The extent to which Hamlin strove for excellence in his horse enterprises, and the money he invested, was without equal at the time.

Nightingale was raised with the crop of colts—about one hundred that year—and began training under the direction of Horace Brown and W. J. Andrews. She made her first appearance close to home as a fresh three-year-old at the East Aurora Fair. She won the 3:00 class in 2:42 1/2 and lowered the mile record for three-year-olds.[159] In September she trotted a $170 purse stakes for three-year-olds, and won all three heats against one other filly in the class. On October 11 at Poughkeepsie, she again placed first in all three heats of a three-year-old stakes race against one other rival.

Nightingale was poised to start her track career out of East Aurora, New York, in the spring of 1889. Heavy rains hit the New

---

157 Ibid., 113.

158 Gordon Davis, "Shades of Ed Geers and Belle Hamlin," *Buffalo Courier*, 1937, East Aurora Town History office files.

159 "East Aurora Fair," *Buffalo Express*, August 29, 1888, 5, fultonhistory.com.

York and Pennsylvania region in late May, culminating on June 1 with devastating floods on a scale never before seen by the inhabitants of the area. While the national news was dominated by the debacle at Johnstown in southwest Pennsylvania, the regions of central Pennsylvania and New York were not spared. Rail lines, roads, and bridges were washed away. Newly seeded crops were lost; livestock, houses, and barns were carried off. People drowned in Tioga County, not just in Johnstown. Railways scurried through the summer to rebuild track and resume timely services for freight and passengers through the Northeast. People cleaned up trash, salvaged what they could, and rebuilt.

In the summer of 1889, Nightingale made an appearance on the third day of the Rochester, New York, Grand Circuit meeting. She came in third out of four competitors in a class for four-year-olds on August 14. The following week she went to nearby Hamburg, New York, and won only the first heat out of five in a 2:30 class. Ending up last of the three, she was not yet meeting Hamlin's expectations for her.

In the summer of 1890, she started trotting on the Grand Circuit in earnest. She began in Mt. Morris, New York, on July 17, and continued on to the Grand Circuit meet in Buffalo for the sixth of August. By mid-August she competed for purses of $1,000–$1,500 in the 2:25 class at the Rochester meeting. Another mare bred at Wood's Deerfield farm, Nightingale's "aunt," Mamie Wood, was entered by Thomas S. Flood at Rochester, though seldom in the same heats. From there Nightingale went to Poughkeepsie, New York, for a week and on to Hartford, Connecticut, by August 29 for similar times and purses. She did a 2:25 1/2 at Hartford as a favorite but did not win. September 5 found her in Springfield, Massachusetts, with

Mamie Wood again, while they both went to Philadelphia trotting in different classes during mid-September.

At Lexington, Kentucky, on October 14, Nightingale ran away. Driven by Andrews from Village Farm, she was the strong favorite to win the 2:26 class, which had a $1,000 purse. She placed midway down the field in the first three heats. Andrews was getting her ready for the fourth heat but was not yet seated in her sulky when she spooked and took off. According to the news account, she became frightened at the "electric cars" (streetcar trolleys that had loud, clanging bells) and got loose from Andrews, "running amongst the trees and finally to her stall with the wreck of a sulky dragging at her heels."[160] Highly strung by nature, she was more difficult to handle after that. Another track writer said she was troubled by "excitement in company."[161]

In 1891, Hamlin hired Ed "Pop" Geers (1851–1924), one of the top drivers on the Grand Circuit, to take his batch of Village Farm horses on the road. At the time, a wealthy horse owner involved in the sport would put out a "stable," a group of ten to twenty horses, on the road. Geers liked to ship his horses south to Alabama or Louisiana for spring training in warmer climates, like baseball teams. The horses were entered at the beginning of the summer in the large venues including the Grand Circuit, such as Cleveland, Buffalo, Springfield, and Philadelphia. By the time the Grand Circuit kicked off in July, the trainers had pared down the number of horses to the best ten or twelve, shipped the nonperformers back home or sold them, and boarded the train. With grooms, sulkies,

---

160 *Clark's Horse Review*, vol. II., No. 21, November 1, 1890, 694, print copy. This journal later was published as *The Horse Review*.
161 "Timely Trotting Topics," *New York Times*, September 13, 1891, NYPL News Archive.

feed, and equipment, they loaded up railcars fitted with stalls and shipped out on the "campaign" trail, the schedule they followed until early October. There was a summer series of race meets, followed by a fall series of meetings as well.

Pop Geers was a Tennessee native and drove both trotters and pacers. He handled horses for several owners at a time, and he owned a couple of his own as well. As long as they were headed to the same city, they shipped out together. In the spring of 1891, when Hamlin engaged the services of the talented Geers, it was not like the movies where the new trainer took a pail of carrots and went to meet the pupil and make friends in her home stall. Geers was already on the train with his string of horses, and Hamlin's group, including Nightingale, merely rendezvoused at whatever city they agreed to join up.

Jittery by this time and carrying some bad habits, Nightingale needed careful handling. Geers was the fellow with the experience and temperament to turn her around. He made several changes for the mare. He was a firm believer in the old horsemen's adage "no feet, no horse." Over a period of weeks, he painstakingly got her hoofs in better condition and tried various shoes until he found the style that fit her correctly. He also experimented with a different bit to stop her fidgeting, and when he started driving her consistently, she began to get faster and also to get over her "cranky notions."[162] Under his training, she settled down that season and showed speed and ability over longer distances.

Geers's status as a legendary horseman has been secured in a century of harness literature. A quiet guy who liked to ride a bicycle,

---

162 Geers, *Ed. Geers' Experience*, 74.

he warranted a bit more coverage as part of this narrative courtesy of G. W. Gocher's 1928 classic, *Trotalong*:

> Geers did not make a spectacular figure in the sulky. Wearing a black cap and jacket he sat rather low, leaning forward. As a rule all of his horses were good mannered and raced from behind. A shift of the bit or a light tap of the whip appeared to be all of the encouragement given to any of them in a close finish but like good ball players they looked for the signal and gave him all that they had without being punished. The mutual understanding which existed between Geers and his horses was one of the mysteries of the turf and made him in reality the Silent Man from Tennessee.

> C. J. Hamlin and Geers had many a battle the first year or two that they were together. Both of them were very positive men. Both had ideas of their own in the matter of balancing and rigging a trotter or pacer. In the end Geers won. When Mr. Hamlin ordered a change Geers let the horse remain idle or told Mr. Hamlin to handle him himself. Finally the Buffalo magnate surrendered, satisfied that Geers was a master. In time he became one of his pupils. . . .

> . . . Geers' imperturbable temper made him an ideal race driver. He never was excited but ever on the alert to take advantage of an opening. He knew all the tricks of the trade and it took a wary driver to outgeneral him in the handling of a horse in a race.

Geers was the first to let his rivals make the pace and break the wind for him. He got the idea from riding a bicycle.[163]

Nightingale proved her endurance in late August of that year in the $10,000 Charter Oak Stakes in Hartford, Connecticut. She beat out two horses from the West Coast, Abbie V. and Little Albert, in a grueling race that took nine heats and two days to finish. The first mare ever to win that lucrative stakes race, she established herself as a premier example of the offspring of her sire, Mambrino King, and the lineage of her dam, Minnequa Maid, from Old Dan back in Pennsylvania.

E. F. GEERS DRIVING NIGHTINGALE SOMETIME AFTER 1892. (PHOTO "NIGHTINGALE-GEERS TM 1314.51" COURTESY OF THE HARNESS RACING MUSEUM AND HALL OF FAME, GOSHEN, NEW YORK, USED WITH PERMISSION.)

---

163 W. H. Gocher, *Trotalong* (Harford, CT: W. H. Gocher, 1928), 83, 85.

The following year, 1892, Nightingale again shone brightly when, at Charter Oak Park in Hartford, Connecticut, on August 23, she took the 2:19 class in three straight heats.[164] Driven by the capable Geers, Another of her accomplishments for 1892 was her two-mile record of 4:33 1/4.[165]

The new rage at the time was the bicycle, and Geers's love of cycling was about to change the sport of harness racing:

> Geers differed in his profession from almost any other man who follows it. At all times up to the close of his career he was eager to learn from the other fellow. It did not make any difference who made a suggestion; if it looked good to him he tried it.

> In 1892 Sterling Elliott made the first bike sulky. He sent it after a few trials to Budd Doble and asked him to try it with Nancy Hanks. A meeting was in progress at Detroit when the cumbersome looking vehicle arrived. Doble hesitated. Geers came along and borrowed it. Honest George was worked a mile to the bike. Geers saw that he could step three or four seconds faster to it than he could to the high wheels. Ed said nothing but on race day borrowed the bike again. He won on a jog. After he repeated at Cleveland the following week the high wheel sulky disappeared over night.[166]

---

164 Wallace's Year Book, v. 8, 1892.
165 Wallace's Year Book, v. 11, 1895.
166 Gocher, *Trotalong*, 84.

With some of the new bike sulkies weighing in at a mere thirty-five pounds and their pneumatic tires and wire spokes giving much less resistance, Geers's—and shortly after, everyone's—horses were flying faster and faster around the tracks. Old records dropped at all the meets, from Massachusetts to California.

Becoming known for her speed over long distances, Nightingale lowered the previous three-mile record to 6:55 1/2 in the fall of 1893 in Nashville, Tennessee. Her three-mile record remained unbroken when harness racing regulations did away with longer-distance contests. According to Geers, one of her best overall performances of 1893 was the Consolation Race at Buffalo, New York, for a purse of $7,000. This endurance battle against four other horses—the gelding Greenleaf, a celebrated peer, Alix, and another black mare of the same name, Nightingale—was extended into seven heats: 2:12 1/4, 2:12, 2:12 1/2, 2:13 1/2, 2:14 1/4, 2:14 1/4, and 2:18. She won the fourth, sixth, and seventh heats.[167]

In 1894, her reputation for "gameness" and longevity over distances had gained her a popular following, and the harness world began to speculate about a match race that would pit her against another well-known distance horse, the midwestern stallion named Greenlander, from Evansville, Indiana. Who would win such a contest? Expectation rose as a date was set for this special event to take place during the Grand Circuit at Buffalo on August 9, 1894. It would go down like this: three miles, best two out of three heats, for a purse of $3,000 cash.

Ahead of time there was plenty of hype: "Both horses are in magnificent condition. They are so evenly matched that there is not likely to be much betting on the event. Nightingale should win the

---

167 Geers, *Ed. Geers' Experience*, 75.

race. Greenlander has not developed anything starting this season so far, while the Buffalo mare has been most carefully prepared. Still the unexpected may happen, and the purse or the long end of it may go to Evansville."[168]

Afterward, the *Spirit of the Times* reported, "The two mile match was not the sensation it was expected to be, as unfortunately the brown stallion, Greenlander, was in no condition for such a race. Nightingale, on the other hand, was in capital condition, and in the first heat she broke the two-mile race record by 11 ½ seconds. As she won by four lengths it is safe to assume that had Greenlander been able to push her out she could have made the time 4:35. She now holds this and the three-mile record, which certainly stamps her as one of the greatest mares of the age."[169]

Another take on it went like this: "There was only one heat in the match, two-mile heat race, between Nightingale and Greenlander. The former won the first as she pleased and could have shut out the Canadian[sic] stallion. Greenlander went lame and Nightingale jogged the second heat alone. Time 4:36 1/2, 5:01 1/2."[170]

Other horses, like Nightingale's peer Alix, the rising star filly Fantasy, and Village Farm's other consistent money-earning pacer, Robert J., also made the race columns that week.

At the Wood farm in the Cowanesque Valley, August brought a new baby to the home of Joseph and his wife, Myrtilla. Soon to be grandparents, they became in their middle age parents once again. Their

---

168 *Buffalo Evening News*, August 9, 1894, 4, fultonhistory.com.
169 August 18, 1894, fultonhistory.com.
170 *Wyoming County Times*, August 16, 1894, fultonhistory.com.

fourth and last child, Russell Wood, was born in the late evening of August 11, 1894. The farm would move on, from horses and tobacco to tractors and dairy cows, under Russell's ownership in the era to come.

In the late fall of 1894, Geers decided he wanted to try wintering his string of horses in the balmy climate of California instead of his usual Selma, Alabama, locale. He called this an experiment. Nightingale and the pacing star Robert J. were among the batch loaded on the train and shipped out to Fresno. There had been an ongoing rivalry between Hamlin with his pacer Robert J. and the owner of his foremost competitor, the stallion Joe Patchen. Joe Patchen's owner had him sent out there also so the turf contest could continue, they hoped in their favor.

A special meet was set for Christmas Day 1894 in Los Angeles. At this meet Robert J. again beat Joe Patchen. Nightingale also met on the same day her new rivals: a pair of West Coast geldings, Azote and Klamath. Azote was California-bred by Senator Stanford, later to become founder of Stanford University. Klamath was a bay from the unlikely northwestern military outpost of Fort Klamath, Oregon. It was tough to beat them on their home turf, and Azote came out on top that day. Christmas in Los Angeles was just the beginning of a rivalry that was to take shape for Nightingale trotting against Azote and Klamath and between Geers's favorite pacer, Robert J., and the horse known as the Iron Horse, Joe Patchen, in the coming months.

A second match was set to take place at Fresno in February. A spell of rainy weather set in, and each night brought a deluge onto the track so as to make it rock hard the following day and impossible to train, let alone race. Geers and a group of other horsemen, including Joe Patchen's driver, were at a loss as to how to fit the track. At midday they borrowed a flock of sheep each, drove them around the track to groom the surface, and worked the horses in the afternoons. The rainy weather and the sheep-on-the-track routine continued so many days that Geers got tired of looking at and dealing with sheep!

The horsemen finally agreed one evening to hold the contests the next day regardless of conditions: the day dawned with mud ankle deep. Every step of man and horse made a sucking noise, and soon everyone was so covered in mud they all looked the same. When Robert J. and Joe Patchen finally got down to pacing their match, the mud flew in all directions, and Geers claimed his horse, Robert J., got so nervous that he broke gait in the last two heats. Joe Patchen won at last.

Nightingale, however, had a good day trotting in the mud at Fresno; she topped both Klamath and Azote in all three heats with a best time of 2:13 1/2. Geers wrote, "I won the free-for-all trot the same day with Nightingale, which in part compensated for the defeat of Robert."[171] Geers was truly fond of both the horses. That was the only year he attempted to winter in California. Later he said that he liked the West Coast except for the rain, but it was too far to ship horses out there across the Rocky Mountains, and the South was more convenient.

Nightingale's victory in the special free-for-all in Fresno also marked the start of a solid year for the seasoned gal who was now a ten-year-old professional at her sport. It was to be a year in which she seemed to have no rest at all, working her way through the southwestern regional circuit as the train cars slowly made their way east for the summer. In May she again took all three heats in a free-for-all in Albuquerque, New Mexico, but with a slower time of 2:27.

---

171 Geers, *Ed. Geers' Experience*, 83–85.

June found her in Denver, Colorado, starting in the 2:11 class and placing third behind her familiar rival, Klamath, and then in Des Moines, Iowa, where she won. LaCrosse, Wisconsin, saw her second to Klamath again, while in Saginaw, Michigan, she was not at her best.

She was midway down a field of six in the 2:11 class in Detroit, Michigan, on July 25, which to no one's surprise was taken by Klamath. One wonders if she or Geers got tired of looking at Klamath's tail end each week, like the old cliché "Unless you're the lead dog, the scenery never changes."

Moving east to Cleveland, Ohio, by August 1, she once more finished well down a large field after Klamath. Joe Patchen, the pacer, was also on hand that day in Cleveland to do a free-for-all. Geers's horses had not seen him since February back in Fresno. Joe Patchen's owners were determined to put their pacing stallion in the limelight, and Joe was doing stud service as well as racing that season. One foal he sired that spring was to become in a few short years the harness icon of all Americana: Dan Patch.

The end of August found Nightingale in New York City at Fleetwood Park, where she perked up and won all three heats in a field of eight. Her times were dropping, and just when it seemed she was tired out, washed up, she made a clean sweep of the 2:10 class in Fort Wayne, Indiana, on September 24, winning all three heats in a large field! She not only got her second wind, she caught fire: in Terre Haute, Indiana, the following week, she won three of five heats with a best time of 2:08! That mile trotted on October 3 would stand as her best for the records. Put in a faster class of 2:09 in Lexington, Kentucky, on October 9, she took first in all three heats there. She stayed in Lexington the next week for a free-for-all against only one opponent and beat a stud colt of the acclaimed Kentucky stallion Nutwood named Lockheart—Nutwood's colt Nutbreaker was the two-year-old Kentucky colt whose record Mamie Wood beat in 1886—to win in three straight heats a $2,000 purse. Her best time that day was 2:09 1/2. Her campaign season was wrapped up on a high note, and she had proved herself worthy as a Village Farm product and a credit to her breeding on both sides.

She went home to East Aurora for a couple of months, then headed with sixteen other horses by rail to Selma, Alabama, for the winter. In early May, she was with a batch that Geers took up to Louisville, Kentucky. Looking toward the summer circuit, they were training at the Louisville Fair & Driving Park track ahead of the season. Geers had her out on the morning of May 15, 1896, for a mild three-minute workout when she collapsed on the track and died immediately. Her heart stopped during a routine she had done hundreds of times. This mare with a stellar reputation for giving all she had, again and again, year in, year out, had finally given her last. She was eleven years old, and her previous season had been her best.

Geers telegraphed Hamlin the news, to which C. J. Hamlin's son, Harry Hamlin, responded with a statement for the press: "Probably Mr. Geers takes her death more to heart than we do. With us a dead horse is a dead horse, while Geers regarded the animal as a pet. We have nothing at present to put in Nightingale's niche, but will fill her place as soon as possible."[172] He continued that their intention had been to retire the mare at the end of the current season. Business was business, horses were money, and the grooms and drivers were the ones who most keenly felt the loss. It was not an uncommon occurrence in the sport.[173]

---

172 "Nightingale Dead", *Buffalo Courier*, May 16, 1896, fultonhistory.com.
173 Ibid.

Nightingale's popularity was evident as news of her death made the nation's papers and stock journals in the coming days. That the track writers were fond of her was clear: "She might be beaten again and again, but her courage never failed."[174] The gambling folks were also going to miss her: "Well-posted betting men had a ticket on Nightingale in every race the horse entered, for they knew that though she might be the last of the procession she would always respond when called on by her driver."[175] The *Brooklyn Daily Eagle* called her "one of the greatest mares in this country."[176] She was an athlete who had produced consistently for the Village Farm under Geers's skillful handling, and she would be missed by her fans as well. Her achievements were kept alive years later by sports writer Walter G. Kelly in his column "The Wide World of Sport," when he penned of her dam Minnequa Maid in 1902 "dam of Nightingale, 2:08, one of the greatest trotters ever produced at Village Farm."[177]

Whether anyone at the Wood farm back in Tioga County followed the turf journals that year and knew of the demise of Old Dan's most famous progeny is unknown. There was never mention of Nightingale's name among them. Old Dan had been dead for several years, and the breeding of trotting stock had passed from their focus. The Woods were moving on to Jersey dairy cows and paying the bills with steady cash from tobacco crops. Crossbred horse teams still plowed the fields and raked the hay, but Joseph and Will Wood's foray into the sporting horse world was over.

---

174 Ibid.

175 May 16, 1896, <u>fultonhistory.com</u>.

176 May 16, 1896, <u>fultonhistory.com</u>.

177 *Buffalo Courier*, April 3, 1902, <u>fultonhistory.com</u>.

CHAPTER 7

SCAPEGOAT: THE FACE OF A CONVICT

Every great family has a couple of bad apples, and Old Dan's family was no exception. In the midst of successful daughters, sons, and their offspring came one notable stinker. At the swanky Hamlin powerhouse of breeding in East Aurora, the Hamlins in 1891 bred Minnequa Maid, their lovely mare from Knoxville, to another of their homegrown stars, Heir-At-Law. He was a talented competitor, able to trot or pace readily at the request of his driver. He had set records at both gaits. Hamlin expected good things from this foal. After all, Minnequa Maid's older daughter Nightingale was that very season taking off for them on the Grand Circuit.

In 1892, Minnequa Maid foaled a bay colt. Gelded early and prepped for a star career, he began training under Ed Geers. Things did not go well from the beginning. Geers was known for his skill with problem horses and for being able to get the best out of a difficult case, but he never liked the young gelding. The Hamlin staff called the horse Scapegoat or often simply just the Goat. The name and the bias stuck, whether he earned it or just lived up to it. He was fast, but when Geers hitched him for trotting, he would stubbornly pace instead, and when he was rigged for pacing he was determined to trot.

Geers gave Scapegoat quite a bit of time to mellow out and as a six-year-old took him along with his young star brother, Milan Chimes, another of Minnequa Maid's colts that Hamlin had high hopes for, to winter in Selma, Alabama, during early 1898. When Geers trimmed down the season's string for the Grand Circuit from fifty to twenty and shipped them up to Louisville for the spring, it is not known if Scapegoat made the cut. It may have been the last straw for Geers. The Goat showed a scheming, tricky disposition. His favorite stunt was to bolt from the pack he was trotting with, veer off toward the rail fence, get down on his belly, and crawl underneath, dragging the sulky along behind—humiliating at the least and dangerous at most! Geers could not put up with shenanigans like this forever. He shared his low opinion of Scapegoat with a track columnist: "He's got a face just like a convict, and you can't trust him."[178]

Later in 1898, Scapegoat went up for sale, cheap. A Chicago businessman, George Castle, who raced horses as his sideline, bit on the bargain horse. The Hamlins were so eager to be rid of the Goat that Harry Hamlin didn't set a price when Castle inquired about the horse. He said, "Suppose you make an offer."[179] Castle's offer of $500 for such a prestigiously bred animal was embarrassingly low but immediately accepted by Hamlin. He did not know who Castle was, and when he discovered the next day at the track that they shared a mutual friend, J. A. Murphy, (owner of Star Pointer) Hamlin sent Murphy on a mission to offer Castle his money back as an honorable way to get out of the deal, about which Hamlin apparently felt some

---

178 Henry Ten Eyck White, "Gossip of Harness Horses", *Chicago Sunday Tribune*, April 6, 1913, <u>fultonhistory.com</u>.
179 Henry Ten Eyck White, "News of the Trotters," *Chicago Sunday Tribune*, October 1, 1899, <u>fultonhistory.com</u>.

guilt. But George Castle wanted to keep the horse, and he did not want a refund.[180]

Scapegoat had started on the East Coast that summer, pacing in the 2:20 class at Hartford, Connecticut, where he finished at the bottom. It may have been at Hartford that Castle made his deal with Hamlin, because from there Scapegoat went directly to Detroit, Michigan, where he again placed last. In Decatur, Illinois, and Bloomington, Indiana, he made poor showings. The Goat perked up considerably after that, though, winning at his next three venues in those states and ending in the money on October 12 that fall in a 2:24 pacing class. Performing inconsistently in 1899, Scapegoat made poor starts in Detroit and Cleveland during July, did a bit better over a swing through the east and New England in August and September, and then surprisingly made his pacing record at 2:11 1/4 on September 21 in Indianapolis.

For all his faults, the Goat proved to be durable and versatile. In July of 1901, he was back at the trotting gait again, hitting the campaign trail as part of Castle's large contingent. July found him starting out in Peoria, Illinois, and continuing on to towns such as Aurora and Mendota, usually winning second or third money; the steamy days of August saw him trundling over the railway to Cleveland and Toledo, Ohio, where he took second and third money there as well. He continued on in Indiana, earning similar placings there during September.

In Pontiac, Michigan, on September 24, he won the 2:40 class at the trot. Entered in a faster 2:30 class at a place called Bourbon, Illinois, he won all three heats with a best time of 2:25. He won, he won! That day he earned himself a place in the record books for

---

180 October 1, 1889, <u>fultonhistory.com</u>.

trotting and became one of those dual-gaited gems that gets into the Standardbred books both ways. He could not go home to rest just yet, though. He made a jaunt down south, won third money in Memphis, Tennessee, on October 26, and three days later won his class in Columbus, Missouri. The Goat had one more appearance to make before his winter break: third money in Savannah, Georgia, on November 9. Then they took him home to Chicago.

By 1902, Scapegoat's reputation had sweetened considerably, with H. T. White, track columnist for the *Chicago Tribune*, describing his workouts at the home Chicago training park with fond words: "Any one who sees Scapegoat taking his work at the West Side track would never imagine that he had ever been possessed of a wrong idea. He jogs along contentedly at any gait his driver sees fit to set, and in and out of the barn is a cheerful horse, willing to do his best."[181]

Had the Goat turned over a new leaf? Did he find things more to his liking in his new midwestern home?

Scapegoat's attitude suffered at least one relapse in Chicago when, after the winter's rest, he started training again one spring. There was a new fellow in charge that year named Eddie McGrath, a "first class horseman" the columnist wrote:

> But that spring Scapegoat was up to all his old tricks and showed a few new ones he had thought out during the cold spell . . . and one day at the West side track in Chicago, after Scapegoat had exhausted all the patience McGrath possessed and shown he was going to be boss unless somebody tamed him right quick, McGrath headed out into the country with him

---

181 June 15, 1902, <u>fultonhistory.com</u>.

and was gone a couple of hours. When he returned Scapegoat was tamed—and tamed for good. A fence rail helped some, and McGrath had other cogent arguments to present to a horse that would lie down on the track in harness and try to crawl under the fence, sulky and all.[182]

After that, Castle continued to campaign Scapegoat as part of his stable; however, he only made two mediocre starts at smaller venues in Illinois during the summer of 1902. His race career in the years after was spotty at best, but he was used as a road horse until his death in 1913 at the ripe old age of twenty-one. When the Goat died, a columnist recounted:

> The double-gaited horse, Scapegoat, that was bred at Village Farm and that was not a success for Ed Geers, but that afterwards acquired more than a little distinction, died a few days ago in Detroit, aged 21 years. He took a pacing record of 2:11 1/4 and a trotting record of 2:21 without change of rigging. On one occasion in Philadelphia he won two races on the speedway on the same day, one at the pacing gait and one at the trotting gait with no other change of rigging than shifting his toe weights. He set a new record for the course in each race. He was sired by Heir-at-Law (2:05 1/4) out of Minnequa Maid, the dam of Nightingale, 2:08.[183]

---

182 *Chicago Sunday Tribune*, April 6, 1913, <u>fultonhistory.com</u>.
183 "Brushing Up For Trots", *The Illustrated Buffalo Express*, March 16, 1913, <u>fultonhistory.com</u>.

Even though both of Scapegoat's parents, Minnequa Maid and Heir-At-Law, made it into Ed Geers's memoirs along with several siblings, Geers made no mention of Scapegoat. The gelding was no favorite with the man who had one of the most stellar careers in the old-time harness world. But the horse's talent, longevity, and vice became his hallmarks. Scapegoat's checkered image showed the truthfulness of the adage "One man's trash is another man's treasure."

CHAPTER 8

REGINA: LIFESTYLES OF THE RICH AND FAMOUS

Regina was the only offspring of Wood's Hambletonian mentioned by name on the Woods' breeding card advertisements printed for the years 1882 and 1884. The cards were just that, pocket cards to be handed out that let a potential customer know the merits of the stallion, his pedigree, and his prices and terms. Because it was costly to have photographs made and it was not convenient to reproduce one, the stallion's attributes had to sell him by narrative description.

Neither card made mention of Kilburn Jim's or Nancy Hackett's achievements; they listed only daughter Regina as "winner of the three-year-old breeder's stake, at Gentlemen's Driving Park, Morrisania, N.Y., in the time of 2:32 1/4." [184] That time was over the standard, so as a youngster Regina had not yet made the mile time necessary to be registered with the trotting association. The mystery was, what had happened to Regina? Had she died at an early age? She did not crop up in race results, time trials, or articles in the news archives. Her siblings trotted and paced their horseshoes off across the country in vintage race news, while she remained elusive.

---

184 Breeding card advertisement, Knoxville Public Library.

That is, until articles about Mamie Wood in Thomas Flood's stable brought her up again. A couple of horse journal articles detailing Mamie's mother, Mary Ann, also revealed that Regina was a full sister to Mamie, having been sired by the stallion Dan and foaled by Mary Ann in 1878, several years before Mamie Wood appeared. Regina did not achieve much of anything on her own merits, but her sale to one of the most colorful men on Wall Street brought the glory of the Gilded Age, and its pitfalls, to the news headlines for decades.

Frank Work, also known as Franklin H. Work (1819–1911), was the epitome of the American rags-to-riches story. From barefooted Ohio boy to Wall Street stockbroker representing the Vanderbilts, he amassed a fortune during his working life. Centered in New York City, Work and his client, William H. Vanderbilt, maintained a lucrative capitalist partnership and drove the fastest horses they could buy.

When Frank Work first moved to New York City as young man, he became associated with William's father, Cornelius "Commodore" Vanderbilt, when American business was grappling with a new paradigm: corporate ownership and the trade of shares on an open market that would become the Wall Street stock exchange. In the decade before the Civil War, businesses that did not make the shift to corporate structure were left behind in the mind-bending, no-rules economic climate that prevailed. The concept of conflict of interest did not tickle anyone's conscience. Aggressive and tenacious men built their fortunes on the young nation's vast natural resources of coal, iron ore, and lumber or agricultural commodities like tobacco and cotton.

This capitalist structure quickly translated into railroad monopolies and the wealth they secured. Cornelius Vanderbilt's fortune was created running steamships before he turned his eyes to rail-roads. He eventually controlled the New York Central rail system, the main artery pumping lifeblood throughout the eastern United States. Frank Work became his investor and his pal, and played a key role when the Commodore tried to acquire the Erie line as well, the event known as the Erie War.[185]

The men's favorite pastime was a friendly rivalry indulged in by many of their colleagues, driving beautiful and fast teams of two roadsters. Hitched to fancy rigs of all descriptions—four-wheeled coaches or light two-wheeled carts in the summers, and cutters and sleighs in the snowy winters—they raced and chased each other through New York streets, in Central Park, and around the nearby racetracks. After the Commodore died in 1876, Work continued his Wall Street connection with the younger William H. Vanderbilt and drove horses against him as well. This team competition also ranged as a variation at most race meets, where prizes and matches were sponsored for money and boasting rights.[186]

Thomas Flood was a member of the New York State Breeder's Association who sponsored stakes races and involved himself in the events of the group. He took his filly, Regina, named after his little niece Regina Flood Thro (later Keyes) to her debut against other colts her age in the summer of 1881 at the association's meet in Morrisania, New York. Morrisania was home to Fleetwood Park, a private half-mile track operated by an exclusive group calling it-self the Gentlemen's Driving Club. The neighborhood known as

---

185   T. J. Stiles, *The First Tycoon: The Epic Life of Cornelius Vanderbilt* (New York:NY) Vintage Books, 2010.

186   W. H. Gocher, "Amateur Trotting Races Still in Favor After Sixty Years", *The Brooklyn Daily Eagle*, October 29, 1929. fultonhistory.com.

Morrisania later became absorbed into the Bronx Borough of the city, near the first Yankee Stadium.

It was here that the wealthy New York City gentlemen had come to play with their horses as well. Frank Work laid eyes on the pretty bay filly, fell in love, and opened his wallet. Flood sold Regina for $4,050. It was a very nice price for an untested three-year-old, but Work had money to spare. He was that year showing off his acclaimed team of geldings, the chestnut Edward and the bay known as Dick Swiveller, or more often just Swiveller. Work was a guy who loved horses as pets, objects of affection and beauty as well as speed and pride. Regina went to her new home, a luxurious stable on Fifty-Sixth Street near the music theater that would in a few years become Carnegie Hall. The stone stable was an expensive work of art in itself: no cushy detail was spared, from glass dome skylights to massive oak doors and beveled glass windows. It was heated by steam and lighted by interior gaslight fixtures mounted in the walls.

Work intended to put Regina in as a substitute, a stand-in, when one of his cherished team needed a rest. He had unique notions about horses' endurance, ideas that made him different from many horsemen of the time. He wanted to give his horses a rest and would often have his grooms and drivers bring out a fresh horse or team to rest the ones he had been driving in Central Park or in the city. His stable was very near the south entrance to Central Park. Regina did not race for her living; she seemed to have it made as understudy to the famous team of geldings. Edward and Swiveller appeared in a well-known Currier and Ives lithograph commemorating their record of 2:16 on July 2, 1882, at the exclusive Fleetwood Park in Morrisania. The lithograph is widely viewable online, and the original is at the Smithsonian as an American treasure. The driver was the same John

Murphy of Nancy Hackett's ill-fated Utica race, and the same John Murphy of Hamlin's sale to Castle of Scapegoat.

Frank Work was fond of all of his animals, and a news writer described a visit to the stockbroker's elegant barn, when he met Regina as well, in a sugary article titled "Horses That Are Smart: Horses That Love Their Masters":

> On a recent afternoon a team stood harnessed to a light wagon in a stable in Fifty-sixth Street, near Seventh Avenue. The stable is said to have cost more money than any other in this country . . . The horses were blanketed . . . An electric bell struck a sharp note. Every horse in the stable pricked its ears and seemed imbued with new life. Two bulldogs jumped in front of the massive doors that swing on 150-pound hinges. William, better known as Boston,[187] who has charge of the horses, remarked: "Here he is."
>
> A side door opened, and a handsome man who has grown gray in New York walked noiselessly in the direction of the team . . .
>
> "Take off the blankets," said the man. The blankets were pulled off. The horses were Edward and a young bay mare. The man stepped to the horses' heads. The mare rubbed her nose slowly up and down her master's face, and appeared to kiss him. The horse rubbed his

---

187 Boston was most likely an African American groom who had spent his life caring for Edward, and Work hired him to accompany and care for the gelding when he purchased him from his previous owner who lived in Boston, Massachusetts.

head against his master, also seeming to kiss him, and then, when he turned away, snapped with a little show of jealousy at the mare's neck. Hearing the rattle of the harness, the man looked around, remarking, "He's full of fun." At the same time he placed pieces of sugar in each of the horses' mouths. . . . "I love horses, and am kind to them, and they are fond of me. . . . That mare, Regina, hitched with Edward, is very fast. She is a five-year-old. I shall hold her back until she is six, and then I will let her show what she can do."[188]

Later in the article after Mr. Work left the stable with the team of Edward and Regina, the man in charge, Boston, continued about his boss' love for horses: "He never overworks his horses. One day he will drive Edward and Dick, then Edward and Regina, or Dick or Edward singly, and so change and give them all exercise. . . . Mr. Work is very much pleased with the way Regina goes to the pole with Edward. I shouldn't wonder if she turned out a clipper."[189]

Although Frank Work had years of wonderful driving on track and road, Regina took him on at least one wild ride when, in the winter of 1884, she spooked at some boys throwing snowballs in the city streets. According to the *Spirit of the Times*:

Mr. Frank Work had just left his stable the other afternoon, driving his bay filly, Regina, to sleigh, and was passing through Fifty-sixth Street on his way to the Park, when, owing to the very lumpy condition of the snow, his sleigh upset, depositing him on

---

188 "Horses That Are Smart", *New York Sun*, December 5, 1883, <u>fultonhistory.com</u>.
189 Ibid.

the ground without injury. The mare ran away down Fifty-sixth Street, and smashed the sleigh into small pieces, which were scattered along the street, and whipped up by the thugs and thieves of the neighborhood in a jiffy, as well as the blankets and whip. The mare was finally stopped, after running nearly to the river. A piece of the dashboard, twelve inches square, was all that was recovered of the sleigh. Mr. Work immediately returned to his stable, and, having his great team, Edward and Swiveller, hitched up, started for the road, finishing his drive pleasantly and without accident. Regina was somewhat injured, but not materially.[190]

Frank Work sold his seat on the New York Stock Exchange in 1901, retired wealthy, and still loved driving his horses for years after that. He took another wicked ride courtesy of a younger and more dangerous team a few years later. That runaway ended with some minor injuries to Mr. Work, the death of one of his horses, and other injured people and horses who were run over in the melee. He was lucky to survive that wreck.

When he died at age ninety-two in March, 1911, the newspapers estimated his worth at $15 million. When the details of his probate were made public some time later, it was closer to $13 million, but the terms of his will provided specifically for the care and maintenance of his horses at other farms.

It was unlikely that Regina lived that long, and she was not mentioned after the article chronicling her accident. That she lived a

---

190 "Track and Road: New York City", *The Spirit of the Times*, January 5, 1884, <u>fultonhistory.com</u>.

plush life for a horse seemed a given, as Work was not known to sell his horses but would retire them to other farms outside the city to live out their days. Regina never made the 2:30 mile time at a sanctioned race nor qualified for entry into the Standardbred records.

Work was wealthy, and by most accounts a gracious fellow, but difficulty stalked him as well. In 1880, just before he bought Regina, Work's daughter Frances married a titled but penniless Irish nobleman, James Burke-Roche, the third Baron Fermoy, whom she had met on a tour of Europe. Much like the plot from Edith Wharton's novel *The Buccaneers*, it became clear soon after that the Irishman was a fortune hunter. Frances's marriage set in motion a series of troubles that would haunt the family for decades. Frances, her father, her siblings, and her children became entangled in her lengthy divorce, child custody, and estate legal battles that played out in courts on both sides of the Atlantic. Frances Work had frequently made the society pages of the city papers, and the family's woes were recounted in the headlines as well. Frances's son, known as Maurice James Burke Roche, became the father to the doomed Frances Burke Roche Spencer Shand Kydd, the mother of equally-tragic Diana Spencer, Princess of Wales.

The details of how both mother and daughter became pawns in a political and royal social-climbing scheme hatched in Britain make the intrigues of *Wolf Hall* seem not so far in the past. Cast in the self-made American capitalist mold, Frank Work was outspoken in his disdain for Europeans who wanted American money. Although he did not live to know it, he became the American ancestor of the most visible contemporary woman of the later twentieth century.[191]

---

191 John Pearson, *Blood Royal: The Story of the Spencers and the Royals*, (New York: New York), HarperCollins Publishers, 1998.

More than twenty years after her death, Diana's face is still there in the grocery checkout aisle. The magazines that endlessly analyze her glamorous albeit troubled life seldom mention her great-great-grandfather Frank Work. Her American ancestor who built himself a fortune during America's Gilded Age. Her American ancestor who bought, drove, and loved a pretty bay mare bred in the Woods' barn in Deerfield.

CHAPTER 9

SNOW ON THE RAILROAD

Like much of American life at the turn of the century, the Grand Circuit depended on the railroads. The best trainers would contract to take on horses for several owners. One of those men at the top of race training during this era was from Whitesville, New York, then known as Spring Mills. William L. Snow (1861–1933) started training racehorses in that village and soon moved his training stable to the busy Erie hub of Hornellsville, New York. Snow was listed in the 1906 Hornellsville City Directory as a "horse trainer" located at 19 Union Street.[192] Around the turn of the century, extant details of his life on the road with his horses revealed the daily routine of campaigners on the harness circuits.[193] Snow had clients from his hometown and as far away as Lexington, Kentucky. Snow also drove Mamie Wood for Thomas Flood a couple of times after Dunham's misadventures (see chapter 5).

With assistant drivers and grooms, he could handle up to two dozen horses for the summer race season. That number of horses and their sulkies, training carts, harnesses, trunks, and feed pails filled two railcars. They also had to haul along some hay and grain, pitchforks, shovels, and oil lanterns.

---

192 *Hornellsville City Directory for 1906*, Hornell Public Library,.
193 Snow v. Wathen (NY App. Div., 4th Dept., October 4, 1905).

The trainers sometimes rented livestock cars, which they fitted out with partitions to separate the horses. Others leased a palace horsecar that was already fitted with about eighteen stalls, padded walls, opening alleyway gates, water tanks, feed mangers, and stow room above the animals for the men to sleep. The palace horsecars might be leased for the season or rented for one trip; then the trainer paid the railroad company for the shipping. The horses were shipped by express, with passenger cars, so they didn't have to wait hours on a siding in the heat for an engine or get injured in plain freight cars. It meant that their trips were hours, or days, shorter than if they were shipped by freight. It was also more expensive.

PALACE HORSECARS COULD BE LEASED FOR A SEASON OR RENTED FOR A SINGLE TRIP.[194]

Snow left his home stables in Hornellsville around the first of May and headed to his favorite spring-training venue at Columbus, Ohio. There he rented stalls for his horses, set up shop, and trained seriously. To get his horses in shape for the circuit, he jogged them at an easy slow pace six or seven miles about four days a week, and gave them each a fast workout at their ability one or two days each week.

---

194 *The Horse Review* v. XII, no. 8, August 20, 1893, 1235.

This regimen he followed during May and June. After the beginning of July when the Grand Circuit kicked in, they traveled almost each week, loading up and heading out to the next city to settle into the track stables there and put in a couple of workouts before the next race meet started.

During the racing season, Snow hired extra men so each horse had his own groom to bathe him, walk him, cool him out, feed and water him, and blanket him after each day's work. These fellows were called "rubbers" or "swipes" for the work they did rubbing down the horses with liniment and wrapping their legs. With the flat-rate horse shipping fee, the railroad company allowed five or six men to travel and sleep with the horses in the express car. The extra swipes often rode along in there, but if the conductors came in to inspect, the trainer had to pay passenger fares for the extra grooms. It was routine that they tried to save money this way.

Around the turn of the century, prices ran something like this: rental for an Arms Palace Horse car was \$32 for a single trip from East Aurora outside Buffalo, New York, to Cleveland, Ohio, and the freight charge to haul the car was \$11.25.[195] At that time, the fastest tracks were considered to be the ones at Columbus, Ohio, Lexington, Kentucky, Readville, Massachusetts, and Providence, Rhode Island. Two express cars to ship nineteen horses from Columbus to Detroit cost Snow \$250. Twelve horses in one car shipped from Providence, Rhode Island to Hartford, Connecticut, cost \$75.[196] Snow paid his men about \$25 per month, and the trainer had to buy other supplies like roll cotton to wrap legs, heel salve to keep hoofs and feet moist from cracking, a leg wash called Tweeds, rubbing alcohol, witch hazel, and an antiseptic tincture called arnica. The Tweeds wash was a

---

195   Ibid.
196   Ibid.

preparation that came in gallon jugs, which Snow bought by the case and used to wipe down the horses after their workouts.

Snow in 1903 charged his clients like this: at home in Hornellsville, they paid $25 per month per horse for training and board. During the May 1 to July 1 training season, they paid $60 per month per horse. Once the group started traveling the circuit in early July, the price went up to $60 per month per horse plus expenses incurred for that animal, like race entrance fees or veterinary care. Costs for feed, board, and extra men were divided equally by the number of horses on the road that month.

Feed prices varied from place to place, and prices were always higher at the track. Snow's horses usually ate about ten to twelve quarts of oats each day, and about ten pounds of hay, which was called "California hay," even on the East Coast. California hay was not necessarily from that state; it simply referred to high-quality grass cured by a humidity-controlled process. Depending on the horses' ages and levels of training, they would sometimes get a bran mash or a little corn. Straw was always needed in large amounts, and because not a lot of feed could be carried on board the railcar, the trainers were at the mercy of what foodstuffs were available at the track dealers'. Often one man was sent ahead on the passenger train to clean, disinfect, and bed the stalls before the horses arrived at the next track.

Sometimes a blacksmith traveled with the stable all summer as well. He would haul his equipment along with a favorite trainer, handle all that stable's shoeing, and pick up extra customers at the race meets as well. A racehorse on the circuit got shoes changed about once a month, and the trainers balanced the horse by putting different weights of shoes on front or back feet to change the length of stride, affecting the horse's gait, speed, and attitude. The shoes and the bit were the most drastic changes a trainer and driver could effect on a horse's handling and performance. Shoes weighed from five to ten ounces apiece and could be made with all kinds of variations to correct problems. There were even complicated shoes with adjustable toe weights that could slide from inside to outside the hoof with the tightening of a screw inside a channel. Another variation was pads to cushion the layer in between the hoof surface and the iron; leather or rubber pads to absorb shock made a difference in comfort that could really put a spring in that horse's step! A set of new shoes with leather pads cost about $3.50 in 1904.[197]

Snow later drove Skeeter W., the pacing descendant of Old Dan from Knoxville, during the season of 1923. Owned at the time by the men known as the Bath Quartette, she thrived

THE EUREKA TOE-WEIGHT. IMPROVED FOR 1877.

G. Knox.   Grafton.

THE | BOSS.

Toe-Weight and "Gilbreth Knox" Quarter Boot. See cut $9 00
Toe-Weight and "Sea Foam" or Box-Quarter Boots 8
Toe-Weight and "Grafton" Quarter Boots. See cut 8 50
Toe-Weights with Heel Guard Straps 5 50
Toe-Weights with Two Set Straps, one around and one under foot, avoiding all heel pressure.. 5 00
Pocket Toe-Weight, the "Boss," seven sets weights in one, 4, 6, 8, 10, 12, 14, or 16 oz., at will.. 5 50
The same with Heel Guard Straps 6 00
Two Extra Sets Weights, per pair 2 25
One set Metal Toe Weights, $3.50; two sets, $5.50; three sets, $7.50; four sets, $10.

Recommended and used by Robert Bonner; W. H Peck; Col. Pepper. Kentucky; Col. Edwards, President, Cleveland Club; A. J. McKimmin, Manager of Blackwood Jr.; J. Cairn Simpson, California; C. S. Green; Budd Doble: Mike Gooding, and nearly all of the prominent drivers.

Send for Circulars to

H. D. McKINNEY, Patentee, Janesville, Wis.

The Superlative METALLIC TOE AND SIDE WEIGHT

FOR ROAD & TROTTING HORSES.

This newly-invented Toe and Side Weight is entirely Metallic, and is the only weight ever used without straps or buckles. This Weight can be used on the track or road, in mud or snow, without loading down or injuring the weight. This weight is held on the foot with a small steel screw, which passes through the shoe and into the spur on the weight, holding it perfectly solid. The side weight is working wonders in improving trotters, causing them to open out wide behind when speeding fast; also, in curing horses that knee knock, hitch, click, interfere, or single foot. This weight is being used by the best horsemen in the world, with perfect success.

All sizes, from 3 oz. up to 14 oz. Toe and Side Weights PRICE.—Single pair, $3; Two pairs, $5; Five pairs, $12. Liberal discount to dealers. For full particulars send for circulars. Address

SETH GRIFFIN, Elyria, O

Agents for New York,

C. M. MOSEMAN & BRO., 114 Chambers Street.

VINTAGE ADVERTISEMENTS SHOWING THE PLACEMENT OF TOE WEIGHTS ON HORSESHOES.

---

197 Ibid.

on the Grand Circuit piloted by Snow's expert hands. By that time Snow had settled in Broome County, New York, in Endicott.[198] He became manager of the Endicott racecourse in his later years, and died in 1933.[199]

That William L. Snow should rise to the top as a trainer on the old Grand Circuit brought pride to the rural farming folks of western New York State. It also showed the strength of harness horse culture which overspread the counties of Allegany and Steuben next to the Pennsylvania border. Snow's routine on the circuit was much like what most of the offspring of Old Dan followed. Each horse had one job: win enough prize money to pay the bills. If some thought Kentucky or Buffalo held the monopoly on success on the many harness racetracks that dotted the nation at the turn of the century, they soon found out that they could be beaten by horsemen and horses who rode the rails out of the train depots at Whitesville, Wellsville, or Hornellsville, New York.

---

198 *Corning Evening Leader*, June 29, 1923, <u>fultonhistory.com</u>.
199 *Cohocton Valley Times-Index*, January 3, 1934, <u>fultonhistory.com</u>.

CHAPTER 10

THE ROAD FROM FARMINGTON: HARRY KEMP

While Mamie Wood and Nightingale were traveling the Grand Circuit in 1890, their fleet-footed roan relatives back in Tioga County raced on the roads. Harry C. Kemp (1868–1961), a farmer who spent his life in Farmington Township, near Deerfield, left a memoir richly peppered with his adventures driving horses.[200] A pious Presbyterian, Kemp didn't spend time at the track, but some of his best road horses were roans that came from Joseph Wood. His family had a farm along the Cummings Creek road in the rolling hills south of the village of Nelson in the Cowanesque Valley, just a few miles east of the Woods' place. Harry grew up raising potatoes and wheat, making butter, and tapping maple trees for syrup. He lived about halfway in between the two best trotting stallions in the county and was one of those many local fellows who bought horses sired by Wood's Hambletonian in Deerfield and by Warwick Boy in Tioga.

He helped his father break the young "Hamiltonians" (Kemp's spelling) to drive. A confident young fellow, he would take over when the spirited colts would rear up and go over backward and his father

---

200 Harry C. Kemp, *Kemp's Life Story*, (New York: Carleton Press, 1960).

lost his nerve. He trained several of these feisty, green colts: "The untamed horses were the ones I liked the best. We had some splendid driving horses . . . At that time we were raising colts from Joseph Wood's famous horses and O. B. Lowell's great trotting Warrick's [sic: Warwick Boy's] at Tioga."[201]

One day in 1890, he hitched his team of young roan colts to a light wagon and announced at the breakfast table he was going to run errands in Elkland. His mother, in spite of her fear of riding with him when he drove the colts, insisted on going along to visit relatives. They headed north down Cummings Creek to Nelson, then turned west and took the Barney Hill Road along the north side of the valley toward Elkland. Kemp let the roans go along at a good clip, and his mother was enjoying her ride. When they crossed the road bridge at Barney Hill, they came upon three horses hitched to sulkies that were starting a road race to Elkland. Harry's mother, much to his surprise, urged him to take them on and see what his roans could do!

His horses had been chafing at the bit, and when they saw the other horses they did not want to be left behind. Harry gained on the racers, and as he pulled close behind them, he gave his colts a little of the whip to urge them on. The other drivers were whipping their horses as well, and as the road came into Elkland, it widened, allowing Harry to come around them, and—all whipping and flying—he got ahead of the three racers by the time they came to the crowd of people who were waiting and cheering in front of the old Case House. "They jumped out of the way as we came by. The little roans were a long way ahead."[202] The Case House was the Greek Revival hotel where Whitcomb/Learn Ford was before Acorn Market gas

---

201 Ibid., 36, 48.
202 Ibid, 49.

station was built at the red light. Kemp continued on without stopping until he got to his uncle's house, where he cooled off his horses. His uncle came out and told him he had ruined the other men's contest and that he should not stay around town right then because no one would pay the bets they had made before he had barged into the race with his roans. One of the men he had beaten was the town's esteemed constable, Lewis Fenton, who had fought in the Civil War and was known for his exploits with horses and law enforcement.[203]

Although he did not give more details about his colts, Kemp's description of them as roans made it likely that they were indeed from Old Dan. Since the Woods' horse passed on the roan coloring as a dominant trait and Warwick Boy was a chestnut not known for throwing roans, it was likely that those particular colts were purchased from Joseph Wood. Joseph had a barnful of good, registered roan colts for sale during the late 1880s. Could these have been Davie C. or Pactolus B.?

Wealthy, colorful men took competitive offspring of Woods' horse across the nation for pride and money, while local fellows enjoyed the spirit and fire of the Hambletonians on the dirt roads close to home. These horses brought thrills to their owners near and far, no matter their place on the social scale. That a common farmer and peer to the Woods loved his fast colts—and got into mischief with them—was a wonderful counterplay to mares like Mamie Wood and Nightingale, who endlessly rode the railways and headlined the race columns in the papers that year. The allure of fast horses was not wasted on the young fellow from Farmington: "With a good horse to drive, I could always get a nice girl to go places with."[204] A century

---

203 Lee Stoddard, "Bold Robbers", *Elkland Journal*, no. 27, July 6, 1977.
204 Kemp, *Life Story*, 36.

later, it would be a muscle car, but in 1890, Harry Kemp knew the appeal of a fast horse.[205]

205 Note: Harry Kemp's son, Roscoe, became a Tioga County commissioner, and his grandson, Robert M. Kemp, served several terms as county president judge during the 1970s.

CHAPTER 11

THE WOODS' TURN OF THE CENTURY

As the year 1900 approached, things began to change in the horse racing world. Baseball leagues, football teams, motorcars, and a myriad of other social pastimes displaced harness racing from the spotlight of American spectator sports. Trotting horses had competition from all kinds of new entertainment. Times were changing, and the Grand Circuit saw its own share of changes around the turn of the century. The race meets left Utica, New York, first, in 1888. A crackdown on gambling in Springfield, Massachusetts, closed the racetrack at Hampden Park in 1893. Rochester Driving Park lapsed in the late 1890s.

Hamlin's Buffalo Driving Park, where horses from the Woods' place had thrilled crowds at the Grand Circuit races for nearly twenty years and also competed as part of the Great Buffalo International Fair, suffered a succession of fires from which it never recovered. Speculation notwithstanding, a small news piece in the farmers' periodical the *Turf, Field, and Farm* from 1897 recounts the demise of the great old racecourse:

Unmerciful disaster follows fast and follows faster the Buffalo track. Its third great conflagration occurred last Saturday night, and was the worst of all, entirely destroying the grand stand and judges' stand, which cost about $25,000 to build, and on which there was no insurance. The entire loss falls upon Mr. Hamlin. The flames could not, as the horses can, burn the track up, hence they left that, but it was about all they did leave. The stands burned like tinder, and the firemen could do nothing but protect adjacent property. All the conflagrations at the track have begun about the same time in the evening, and are certainly the work of an incendiary, probably some fanatic who is opposed to racing. Mr. Hamlin's pocket is deep, but these repeated drafts on it must be growing tiresome.[206]

C. J. Hamlin was growing old, and even his wealth could not roll back the years. He did not rebuild the park. A few years later, the tract of land was sold for residential development, which would become known as the Hamlin Park neighborhood of Buffalo.[207]

Fleetwood Park closed in 1898. The area was by that time becoming known as part of the Bronx, and streets were rerouted over portions of that old track.[208] It was very near where the first Yankee Stadium was built.

---

206 Hamilton Busbey, *Turf, Field and Farm*, vol. LXIV, no. 1, January 1, 1897, 7, Hathitrust Digital Library.

207 Mark Puma, "The History of Hamlin Park Part IV: Hamlin's Driving Park and the Home Builders," *Buffalo Rising*, August 21, 2013, https://www.buffalorising.com/2013/08/the-history-of-hamlin-park-part-iv-hamlins-driving-park-and-the-home-builders/.

208 Kevin Walsh, "Forgotten New York", https://forgotten-ny.com/2011/01/morrisania-bronx/.

Of the original venues, Cleveland, Ohio, moved its Grand Circuit race to North Randall, Ohio (where Chilcoot would begin his career), until the 1940s, and Charter Oak Park in Hartford, Connecticut, hosted meets into the 1930s. The first state fair to host a Grand Circuit race was the New York State Fair, which entered the Grand Circuit in 1901.

In 1908 the New York legislature passed antigambling laws that made it a crime to be involved with betting in any way. Gambling associated with running horses as well as harness racing had a strong current in the state, and the governor was determined to clean it up. The Grand Circuit moved north of the border to Fort Erie, Ontario, for a few years; then the circuit lapsed from the region completely.[209]

Before the century turned, Joseph Wood's older sons Fred and Perry grew to adulthood. Stories passed down through the family related some of their adventures as young fellows courting with double dates driving horses and buggies. Steam and horsepower gave way to gasoline engines. New technology and optimism propelled all manner of new farm machinery; daily life and farm work changed with astounding new inventions each year. Railroads dominated commerce and set the tone for social schedules. There were still exciting horse races at the local fairs, but new tractors and motorcars were the rage for most young folks.

---

209 Davis, "Shades of Ed Geers."

PICTURE POSTCARD, KNOXVILLE MAIN STREET LOOKING EAST AROUND 1900. BILLY THE CLOTHIER LEFT SIDE, STREET FLOOR, DR. SMITH, DENTIST, SECOND FLOOR. ADAMS HOUSE HOTEL, WHICH WAS RUN BY MANY INDIVIDUALS, INCLUDING J. G. WAKELY AND JEROME HATHAWAY, ON RIGHT SIDE WHERE CITIZENS & NORTHERN BANK NOW IS.

Fred married first and moved to his own place. He was an erstwhile shopkeeper—first as partner in Pride & Wood dry goods on Main Street in Westfield, then a feed dealership based out of his home on Knox Road in Deerfield. He then returned his business to Westfield, retailing on West Main Street. Later he moved near the New York Central railroad depot, where his store in time became affiliated with Agway and passed down through his family branch to the present time.

Perry was fond of horses but made his living with dairy cows. He developed a Jersey dairy first on the home farm and built up a retail residential route. He bottled his milk and made deliveries with a horse team and wagon from his folks' place. He then settled on his own farm west of Knoxville in Deerfield Township further up the river road. His family grew large, and several branches of that family stayed in agriculture. Edna and Russell grew to adulthood as the new century began, with party-line telephones—local only—and motorcars connecting folks in an ever more efficient way. The ties to New Jersey and New York still connected the older folks to their kin in the old home.

WOOD FAMILY IN THE FRONT PARLOR OF THEIR HOME AROUND 1900. BACK: JOSEPH, FRED, ORA & ELLA YOUMANS WOOD, MABEL WAINWRIGHT, IVAN KELTS. MIDDLE: MYRTILLA, STELLA MOURHESS, HESTER EVERITT WAINWRIGHT, KENNETH KELTS, MELISSA WOOD WAINWRIGHT, JEAN WAINWRIGHT. FRONT: RUSSELL, EDNA. (COURTESY MARYON PAINTER SWANSON, IDENTIFICATION BY MARK WOOD.)

During one summer at the turn of the century, the photographer Thomas Wood made a visit from his Chicago home. He had finally settled down there, remarried, and had two younger children. When he was starting out as a photographer in the 1870s, he had been widowed and found it necessary to leave his little daughter for a few years with his folks, Oliver L. and Thankful, in Knoxville, while he found his footing in his business. He went from Goshen, New York, to Pittsburg and from there to Kalamazoo, Michigan, for a time in the 1880s before making Chicago his home and opening a studio there around 1890 until his death. When he arrived in Deerfield to see his relatives, he brought along his camera, with which he could take wide-angle panoramic views. He gathered before his lens a large group of folks at the Knoxville riverside picnic grove then called Lawrence's Retreat near the confluence of Troups Creek with the Cowanesque. This extended clan included folks encompassing both sides of the house: Wainwrights, Woods, Kelts, Everitts, and others. This bucolic picnic grove would fall victim to the flood in 1916, when it would virtually be swept from the landscape by the post-lumbering deluge.

Thomas took other photographs at the same time: sweeping views of farmhouses with tobacco growing in the fields, the valley from a hilltop vista, and family groups indoors and out. The set of photos, each mounted separately on a distinctive cabinet cardboard and embossed with Thomas's Chicago studio address, was scattered among the family branches, and awareness of him as the family photographer fell from knowledge.

THOMAS E. WOOD, 1893, KALAMAZOO, MICHIGAN.

VERSO OF ELIAS PERRY MASTERSON'S PHOTOGRAPH AND THOMAS E. WOOD'S PHOTOGRAPH. PERRY MASTERSON TAUGHT HIS YOUNGER BROTHER-IN-LAW THE SKILL AND TRADE IN PORT JERVIS.

ELIAS PERRY MASTERSON, PHOTOGRAPHER, MARRIED PHEBE JANE WOOD.

The Woods still raised horses at the turn of the century, although by then cash crops and milk sent to the nearby condenseries supported the farm. The year 1900 may have marked the height of the labor-intensive tobacco culture in the Cowanesque Valley as well. In July of that summer, a fierce storm blew in and lightning struck five horses. They were killed as they huddled together for shelter under a tree.[210]

Joseph and Myrtilla's daughter Edna grew up during the twilight era of the racehorses, having been born the year before the old stallion died in 1888. Like many farm girls, she had a fondness for animals and a special love for horses. Even though Old Dan was no longer a presence in the lovely, big barn, his descendants still grazed the pastures along the river road. Edna grew into an accomplished young lady known for her beauty and gracious nature. She also loved to ride. During the years beginning in 1915, her diary provided a window into life on the Wood farm in the era of the Great War.[211]

By that time, the Woods' home had a gasoline-powered icebox and a party-line telephone but no electricity. Edna had spent a year in upstate New York at college, but heading toward the age of thirty she had not yet married and was still living at home with her parents and younger brother, Russell. Russell was about twenty-one that year, and he had what Edna described as "auto fever." Their teenage nieces, Fred's daughters, already had a motorcar to drive, and he could hardly wait to get one as well.

The farm was still powered by horses, plowing, raking hay, and growing grain such as oats and wheat. Tobacco brought in additional cash each year, but the dairy cows provided the mainstay. In their

---

210 *Wellsboro Agitator*, July 11, 1900, Green Free Library Newspaper Archives.
211 Edna Wood Robbins diaries for years 1915-1918, unpublished. Transcribed and shared by Barbara Robbins Cobb.

first decades in Deerfield, the Woods had made butter right at the farm to preserve their perishable product before quick transport made shipment of liquid milk possible. By 1915, their liquid milk could be quickly cooled, sent to nearby condenseries for processing, and shipped by rail to other markets.

CHEESE FACTORY IN AUSTINBURG, WHERE MANY DAIRY FARMERS SOLD THEIR LIQUID MILK. GRANGE HALL LATER BUILT ON THIS LOCATION. (COURTESY KNOXVILLE PUBLIC LIBRARY.)

Edna's own mare was named Agnes. She rode Agnes to visit her brother Fred's family about four miles each way. Hitched to a buggy, Agnes was driven by Edna often when she went to help her nieces, her sisters-in-law, and her grandmother with sewing clothes, cooking, and preserving. When the berries ripened on the hillside in late summer, Edna crossed the river on Agnes to pick her buckets full. She rode the mare to Knoxville to mail letters. When Agnes needed to be shod, Edna rode her to town to the blacksmith. Her photograph taken in the front yard showed her with a dark-colored horse that may have been Agnes. Edna wore a full skirt, and the horse was saddled with a man's Western-style rig, clearly not a ladies' side-saddle. Her father, Joseph, by this time was nearly seventy, and he often rode horseback with Edna. He rode a mare they called Lucille. Lucille was driven on the road, and both mares were likely descended from Old Dan. There was a team of workhorses and a team of mules on the farm as well.

Folks traveled by train, and Joseph kept ties with family back in New Jersey. He left in May of 1915 to help "Uncle Sam" Christie, his brother-in-law, also by that time an aged farmer, plow and put in crops on his farm there. Joseph stayed for a month and rode the rail line both ways. Russell was holding down the work at home, and the older brothers Fred and Perry with their boys were nearby and lent hands often. Other horses were still being raised on the farm. When the late summer grass dwindled in the pastures across the river in September of that year, several colts broke out as they searched for better grass. Russell had to go over to hunt for them.

Lest anyone view the cycle of farm chores as dull, consider the simple sweetness of a gift given by Edna's mother, Myrtilla, to her son Fred's family: a hen with nineteen newly hatched chicks, a source of eggs for breakfast, custards, and all manner of cooking was flavored with the promise of savory roast chicken and gravy dinners in the future. Russell was tasked with digging his older brother, Fred, a new cesspool, but he hastened the job along by blasting it out with dynamite. Even a country sewer system was made into a special occasion!

EDNA WOOD ROBBINS WITH HER SADDLE MARE, CIRCA
1917. (COURTESY BARBARA ROBBINS COBB.)

SAMUEL AND EMILY WOOD CHRISTIE ON RIGHT WITH UNIDENTIFIED RELATIVES.

Relatives traveled constantly from one farm to another to help with haying, harvest, or butchering. The women sewed, canned fruit, and cooked for one another, and the extended clan with grandparents, in-laws, and grandchildren gathered in one another's homes frequently for meals. Sometimes Edna lent Agnes if someone else needed a ride home. On one occasion she let her nephew, Perry's son Dean, drive Agnes to his own home one evening. Dean's sister, Marjorie, brought the mare back in the morning.

Edna's diary chronicles a time of Chautauqua camp meetings, church socials, hay pressers, threshers, and that most exciting of all days: the arrival of Russell's new "Overland" auto! The worst flood folks had seen since 1889 hit in June of 1916. It washed out railroad trestles, the river bridge south of Knoxville, and the Lawrence's retreat picnic grove, and carried away buildings. Edna rode horseback up the valley to look at the ruins. Fences and crops were gone, fields were torn up, and the trains did not run for days afterward.

That year—1916—up in Ontario, the young colt Chilcoot (son of Chimes Girl, daughter of Minnequa Maid) was starting his racing career trotting on the frozen rivers.

In late 1916, everyone was dismayed to hear that Germany would not accept Russia's terms for peace, and there would be more war. The pastures across the river held up well that year, and Russell did not have to bring the stock off the hill until the middle of November. In January of 1917, there was more excitement when the new tractor arrived. Russell took care of horses on the farm, but his heart was all in the new engine-driven technology. He loved machines, he loved engines, and he loved motorcars.

That spring was about the time that James Grant Wakely from nearby Brookfield took his Wood's Hambletonian granddaughter, a mare named Little Maiden, to be bred to Lockwood Jr., son of Direct Hal, the renowned pacer then owned at Wellsville, New York. Direct Hal was bred and owned by Ed Geers during his time at Village Farm. Geers sold him for $10,000, the stallion's record time was 2:04 1/2.

In April, the day came that everyone dreaded; the United States was getting into the war. "War was declared yesterday morning," Edna wrote on the seventh of April. By June she was going to Knoxville and Wellsboro, to social gatherings where ladies cut and rolled cotton bandages to be sent by the Red Cross to the war effort. When July came, cousin Karl Kelts was drafted; another favorite cousin in New Jersey, Roy Elston, was to go as well. In September, a good friend of Edna's niece, Marjorie (Perry's daughter) named Clarence Bellows, left. They bid him good-bye. The following autumn, Bellows's plane crashed in the Argonne forest in France.

Bellows died in the Allies' last big offensive just a few weeks before the armistice in November. The Great War was going to change everyone's lives.

GROUP OF YOUNG MEN ON MAIN STREET, KNOXVILLE, INCLUDING JAMES G. WAKELY. HE LATER OPERATED ADAMS HOUSE HOTEL WITH ITS LIVERY STABLE AND BRED AND RAISED THE PACING MARE SKEETER W. (PHOTO COURTESY KNOXVILLE PUBLIC LIBRARY.)

Edna got engaged that winter. She was past thirty and apparently so happy at home that she took her time to decide among the several men who courted her during the diary years. She was to marry Earle Robbins, a fellow from Spring Mills, New York, later known as Whitesville. In January 1918, Earle went with her to take Agnes for horseshoes. A few days later when some men driving a car got stuck in the snow near the farm, she lent Agnes to them to drive to town in a sleigh.

Early 1918 found all hands on deck getting the Woods' big house in shape for a wedding: Edna shopped for all manner of clothes and accessories, Mother sewed and cleaned in every room, and Russell fetched the wallpaper hanger from Elkland. Even father Joseph was pressed into service doing a most unmanly chore: scrubbing and polishing woodwork in the front hall. The daughter of the family was finally having a wedding, and the place was going to shine. The horses were sidelined. As the big day approached, the diary fell silent, abandoned.

So as the details of daily life on the Joseph Wood farm faded, Edna's married life began. On the racehorse scene, 1918 became the big year that Chilcoot made his comeback on the Grand Circuit, capping it with a win of the famous Charter Oak Stakes. Up the road at the Wakely's farm, Little Maiden foaled her filly, who would become known as Skeeter W., and would move up into the Grand Circuit to make everyone in the region proud. Edna's love for horses continued even as her life, and everyone's, moved on in a myriad of changing times. It was Edna and her husband, Earle Robbins, who kept connections with the racehorse scene, taking their sons to the trotting track each year.

Edna and Earle took possession of the oil painting of Wood's Hambletonian done by Edna's aunt Rilla Wainwright King and cherished it. When Edna died, Earle donated it, together with its source photograph imprinted with Thomas E. Wood's studio trademark on the back, to the Knoxville Public Library, where it could be admired and enjoyed by the community. Edna and Earle kept a stereopticon image of Nancy Hackett—with the handwritten name on the back—tacked to their wall, keeping alive the memory of her big summer in 1878. Earle kept a color lithograph calendar print of Goldsmith Maid on his barn office wall, with the knowledge of that famous early mare's connection to the stallion in Deerfield. It seemed that for decades folks were not that interested in asking about, or listening to, the horse stories. It is bittersweet to imagine what Edna's or Earle's memories may have lent to this narrative.

WOOD FARM IN 1960s.

Where to leave the Wood farm? With each passing generation, knowledge of the details about the old horses faded. Old Dan, according to family story, was buried at the northwest corner of the big barn. Sometime later they built a silo overtop, then another. There was no single dispersal sale of horses, but oral stories indicated that some of the best horses and rigs were sold to buyers in Whitesville, New York.[212] After World War I, most folks traveled by motor car and the shift from draft horse power to gasoline engines was underway. Horses were cheap.

The farm at Deerfield along the Cowanesque River has seen some changes: dairy cows, beef cows, the end of tobacco, the changing over of buildings and ownership to the current members of the family. The big main barn was remodeled to house a dairy of Holstein cows at least two different times, in the 1950s and again in the 1970s. The farm achieved Pennsylvania's "century farm" designation also during the 1970s, having been used as a production farm within the same family ownership continually since 1861.

During the 1990s, additional acreage was acquired east and west of the main 220-acre tract. The farm entered into another state designation, that of "farmland preservation," with the intent of retaining the land for agricultural use.[213] The busy river road, now known as Route 49 corridor, is a busy two-lane byway, carrying freight and commuters east and west. The hills surrounding the flat valley fields have largely reverted to forest land. The tanneries and lumber mills west are gone; the New York Central railway was taken out in the 1960s, the second railroad known in later years as the B & O or the WAG, lasted until the early 1970s.

A handful of horses, none Standardbreds, reappeared on the farm for riding and driving. A Belgian team driven by the farm's current owner often hauled wagons of folks around the flat fields for summer picnics or reunions during the 1980s into the 2000s. The

---

212 Eleanor Robbins, conversation with the author, 2010.
213 Carolyn Moyer, "Farmland Preservation Grows", *Lancaster Farming*, vol. 46, no. 30, May 26, 2001.

resident Wood horsemen now ride in the western style and can be seen checking beef cows on horseback. If folks want to see harness racing these days they must seek it out. Horse stories come alive in vintage photos, tales told around the picnic table, or news archives.

Harness racing continues today among a myriad of American sports. Enthusiasts can see the big names of the sport at the Red Mile in Lexington, Kentucky, the Hambletonian Stakes for trotters at Madison Square Garden, or the Little Brown Jug for pacers in Delaware, Ohio. The thrill is alive at small fairs all around the nation, from Bath, New York, to Gratz, Pennsylvania, and beyond, where the excitement still pounds down the backstretch with the sound of the horses' hoofs churning up the dust. So many things, however, fill American mainstream life that many never have seen a harness race.

The story of Woods Hambletonian #572, Old Dan, has been a trip back in time. It presents a snapshot of an era when the farm along the Cowanesque Valley river bottom in Deerfield was home to a stallion whose sons and daughters captivated the region. Their wins on the Grand Circuit connected Tioga County to the larger American story. The significance of the stallion known to the Wood family as Dan, later Old Dan, and to the harness world as Wood's Hambletonian #572, was best summed up by the editor of *The Breeder's Gazette* noting the stallion's death for his readers:

A better sire than Happy Medium, when his opportunities are considered, that also died in 1888, was Wood's Hambletonian. He was by Alexander's Abdallah, his dam being a roan mare of whose breeding nothing was known, but that she was an unusually potent animal is shown by the fact that she imparted her color not only to her son but to more than fifty per cent of his descendants. Nearly all of the sons and daughters of Wood's Hambletonian have a good deal of speed at the trot. Their sire spent his life in a portion of Pennsylvania where well-bred horses were a rarity, and that under such circumstances he should have become the sire of so many animals with records better than 2:20 is remarkable, and one of the strongest evidences that, had he lived, Alexander's Abdallah would have proven himself one of the best sons of Rysdyk's Hambletonian, ranking with George Wilkes and Electioneer.[214]

214 "Echoes of the Turf", *The Breeder's Gazette*, vol. XV, no. 3, January 16, 1889, 67, Hathitrust Digital Library.

LEGACY HORSES, OUTLIERS AND ED GEERS

Chilcoot: Keeping Up Family Tradition

Among the many sons and daughters of Old Dan, one broodmare stood apart from the rest: Minnequa Maid, the lovely bay mare that caught C. J. Hamlin's eye and kept his affection until the end. He bragged more than once that she was one of the best bargains he ever acquired among his hundreds of horses. Her job at Village Farm was not to race, but to be a mother, and that she did very well. Her roster goes like this:

1885: Nightingale, by Mambrino King
1887: Hereward, by Mambrino King
1888: Chimes Maid, by Chimes
1889: Chimes Girl, by Chimes
1891: Scapegoat, by Heir-at-Law
1892: Milan Chimes, by Chimes

Chimes Girl was started from Village Farm as a two-year-old, and she promised to be very fast. Handled by one of Geers' assistant trainers named Alonzo McDonald, she so impressed the race columnists that they called her "sensational" after she clocked a flawless

2:26 mile over the Buffalo Driving Park near home.[215] Folks held high hopes that the filly would follow in her big sister Nightingale's success. However, Chimes Girl was prone to injury and spent so much time out with sprains and recurring lameness that one track writer termed her career as "erratic" at best.[216] The mare did double duty for Hamlins, and she had produced three foals for them by the spring of 1895, when they shipped her down south with Ed Geers to train for a return to the Grand Circuit. But she just could not hold up under the rigors of the track and went back to the farm as a broodmare for many years.

In 1905, the aging and ailing C. J. Hamlin consigned most of his horses at Village Farm to a dispersal held at Madison Square Garden. The sale attracted buyers from all over the world to buy his noteworthy stock. Hamlin died just a few weeks later, and the era of Buffalo as trotting horse central began to fade.

Three years later, the younger Hamlin consigned a dozen of the remaining trotting stock to the Tranter Kenney Sale in Lexington Kentucky.[217] Chimes Girl, an aged mare by this time, was among this batch. In Kentucky, she was purchased by Walnut Hall to be a broodmare at that esteemed farm. Several years later she was bred there to the acclaimed stud San Francisco #49173, and foaled the colt Chilcoot in 1912. Chimes Girl was twenty-three years old.[218] Chilcoot was a beautiful, bright chestnut, large and growthy, and he was sold to a Canadian Robert Bennett and taken there to live in Horning's Mills, Ontario.

---

215   "The Sensational Two Year Old Chimes Girl, 2:26", *The Daily Republican*, October 20, 1891, <u>fultonhistory.com</u>

216   "Eastern Harness Racers", *The Sun*, July 17, 1898, <u>fultonhistory.com</u>

217   "Village Farm Shipment", *Buffalo Courier*, March 24, 1908, <u>fultonhistory.com</u>.

218   *Breeder's Journal*, vols. 7 and 8, 1918, Hathitrust Digital Library.

Chilcoot—who likely was given the chilly-sounding Canuck name after his arrival in his new Canadian home—was trained for the track and driven by Tom Murphy. (Was he son of John Murphy from the bygone days of Kilburn Jim and Nancy Hackett?) At four years old, Chilcoot made his debut in Ontario, trotting on ice at the winter meetings in that region often referred to at that time as the Dominion. Horses for the ice racing were equipped with sharp caulks, spikes on the bottom of their horseshoes to provide extra traction for ice and snow. Here, racing was less formal than in the United States, and the horses raced with both bicycle sulkies and with small sleighs or cutters on the snow-covered oval tracks, and also on the frozen river straightaways. Chilcoot was very fast there, but summer trotting opportunities were slim in Ontario because the Canadians were focused on running horses rather than harness racing. So he was brought to North Randall, Ohio, to be trained and started from there.[219]

He did very well the summer of 1916 based out of Ohio. But in 1917 he got injured; the paper said he wrenched his leg when he swerved to avoid a harrow that was being used to groom the track and had been accidentally left in the way.[220] So he made no starts in 1917.

By the summer season of 1918, Chilcoot was in good shape again and ready to return for another round on the American harness circuit. He was called by the track writers the "Canuck whirlwind," and he started that summer out at the North Randall, Ohio, track where he was based with driver Tom Murphy.[221] The big, beautiful

---

219 www.canadianhorseracinghalloffame.com/1976/11/11/chilcoot/.

220 "Noted Harness Racer is Due to Come Back", *Ithaca Daily News*, April 29, 1918, fultonhistory.com.

221 ibid.

chestnut contended with ten other horses on July 8 there and won first money his first time out, his times hovering around 2:07. He blazed through the Midwest that month, winning second money of a $3,000 purse against eight others in Kalamazoo, Michigan, on July 18 and proceeded on to Toledo, Ohio, the next week for another second money finish against ten competitors.

From there Chilcoot went to Columbus, Ohio, for a Grand Circuit class, winning that class in three straight heats. In that race who should be driving against Murphy and Chilcoot but good old Ed Geers, at the reins of a colt named Heir Reaper. Still a force to be reckoned with into advanced age, Geers pushed Murphy and Chilcoot so hard they got the horse's new fastest record, 2:04 1/4!

From there they were off to the Grand Circuit meeting at the Belmont Driving Park, just outside Philadelphia, Pennsylvania, on August 12, where Chilcoot easily took the 2:06 class trot in three straight heats. He won first money of a $1,000 purse there. Ten days later Chilcoot and Murphy met up with Geers again in Poughkeepsie. Geers, driving a colt named June Red, beat Chilcoot that day in a hard-fought race against six other horses. Chilcoot had to settle for second money of a more lucrative $5,000 pot. By this time, Murphy—and others—knew the horse was lame.

Just a few days later, June Red with Geers and Chilcoot with Murphy squared off once more in Readville, Massachusetts. The purse was $5,000 here as well, and there were six other horses entered. The race was named the Massachusetts stake, and Chilcoot won all three heats, topping June Red and Geers. Murphy kept on, taking Chilcoot to Hartford, Connecticut, for the prestigious and pricey Charter Oak Stakes on September 5.

The $10,000 prize loomed large. The big chestnut colt, battling lameness but competitive as always, knew his business when he got on the track. Chilcoot won the first two heats out of three to take the prize. The times, 2:06 1/2 and 2:07 1/2, were not his fastest, but they were enough to get Murphy the win. It was certainly Chilcoot's high-water mark. Murphy announced right away that the stallion would be taken off the Circuit. Chilcoot went out on top; he had been traveling and giving his all with a bowed tendon.

In the headlines celebrating Chilcoot's big victory, he was compared with his famous "aunt," Nightingale, recapping her win of the Charter Oak twenty-seven years before, in 1891! His relatives had set the bar high, and he kept up expectations for the track writers and fans who had not forgotten his forbears' exploits. His speed and endurance were compared with that of Nightingale during the decade of the 1890s, and columnists made fond reference to that mare's stardom during that golden era of the harness horse.[222]

There was some speculation that Chilcoot could recover sound and return to the Grand Circuit, but as a six-year-old he went home to Canada and stayed. With a single stellar season to his credit, he became popular as a stud. His many offspring populated the tracks, on and off the Grand Circuit, in the years following. Some went to Europe, a daughter named Princess Iroquois paced her way to the top at the New York State Fair in Syracuse in 1929, and other daughters, Miss Chilcoot and San Abbess, trotted in Toronto in 1931 and 1934.[223] A couple found their way to nearby Quebec province, and one mare named Sisco paced back close to Pennsylvania at the Hornellsville Fair in 1927.[224]

---

222 "Chilcoot Laid on Shelf," *New York Times*, September 22, 1918, www.nytimes.com
223 *Syracuse Journal*, July 29, 1931, fultonhistory.com.
224 *Evening Tribune-Times*, August 24, 1927, fultonhistory.com.

CHILCOOT RETIRED IN CANADA WITH A SUCCESSFUL BREEDING CAREER. (COURTESY CANADIAN HORSE RACING HALL OF FAME.)

Chilcoot's achievements on the track and as a stallion were lauded in 1976, when he was inducted into the Canadian Standardbred Hall of Fame. Through Chilcoot, numerous strains of Wood's Hambletonian's family trotted and paced their way on down through the decades in the United States, Canada, and Europe.

Skeeter W., the Darling of the Twenties

As Chilcoot retired to his home in Ontario, the generation of Wood horsemen passed on. Horses do not live forever; neither do men. The legacies left behind were the stories, the pictures, and the memories of the ones who came after. Joseph Wood passed away in the year 1920, his family and his farm seeing diverse changes since trotting horses filled the box stalls and pastures there. Old Dan had himself been gone thirty years, the same space he had lived. Yet the legacy of the horse was alive and well, as was the legacy of the farmer.

Within the span of three years, the last four Wood brothers died, the three horsemen and the photographer who chronicled the family in image.

O. H. Wood died in 1917 at age ninety-one, and his family's horse heritage was printed prominently in his obituary. He died in Tioga at the home of his daughter, Catherine (Carrie) Metcalf. She was the wife of Daniel Metcalf, a noted tobacco farmer. The children of O. H. were Julius, who moved to Indiana by 1878 and whose family stayed there; Sarah, who married Jerome Hathaway, O. H.'s erstwhile horse partner; Catherine, who married Metcalf; and Charles M. Wood, who lived north of Knoxville and later in Steuben County and also raced harness horses.

William C. Wood died in 1918, survived by his much younger wife, Nannie, with no children.

Thomas E. Wood died in 1918 in Chicago. His branch's last contact with the family here may have been a letter from his daughter to Joseph and Myrtilla. He had reclaimed his older daughter, LaPette, from his parents with whom he had left her while he moved frequently during the 1870s. He ultimately settled his photography studio in downtown Chicago, where he married a woman named Fannie and had a son, Frank, and a daughter. Thomas and Fannie were buried there, but it seemed the folks in Pennsylvania lost contact with the children.

Joseph Wood died in December of 1920, and his obituary recounted the family's Hambletonian horse legacy. He was seventy-four years old. Myrtilla lived in the big house until Russell married Ruth Edgcomb in 1922; then she moved to town into the house now owned by Leddys on South First Street. Myrtilla was a woman who gathered kinfolk in for dinner, picnics, and church gatherings, a force that held the social fabric of the extended family together.

That year a young three-year-old filly who had been foaled just outside Knoxville came into her own at the track. She was a pacer, and her pedigree through her dam's side back to the Wood farm had stayed local. Skeeter W. was her name, and she was bred and carefully raised by J. G. (James Grant) Wakely (1884-1927) (also spelled Wakeley or Wakley), whose clan resided north of Knoxville toward Austinburg. Wakely was the proprietor of the Adams House hotel, with its adjoining livery stable, in Knoxville. [225]

The filly was trained during the season of 1920 at the Westfield Fairground track by another local horseman, George W. Bottum. Skeeter was entered at the fair races there at Westfield, and at

---

225 J. G. Wakely was often confused with his relative, J. B. Wakely. It was difficult to distinguish between the two men, and several news articles mistook one for the other. The author used the Adams House print letterhead dated 1918 naming J.G. Wakely as proprietor, as authority for this conclusion.

Hornell, Bath, and Elmira in New York. Impressed with her prospects, a group of businessmen from Bath bought her from Wakely. Calling themselves the Bath Quartette Stables, they put Skeeter W. out on the Grand Circuit, where she made them, and the whole region, proud with her many victories during a career that stretched all through the decade.

Even though Joseph Wood and his brothers had passed on, his son Perry's family likely kept up with Skeeter's progress, driving to Syracuse to the state fair to watch the horse races more than once during those years. It took them at least six hours each way to drive north to the fair, but they made a family outing of it. At least once they took a picture of a picnic rest stop on the way, grandbabies and all, in two motorcars. Skeeter's record would stand at 2:03 1/4, made on September 2, 1925, at Milwaukee, Wisconsin.

Skeeter W.'s success on the Grand Circuit was proof of the legacy of Wood's Hambletonian. When she made a special exhibition at the Bath Fair as her "retirement" appearance before heading to her next job of motherhood at a new home in Philadelphia, Pennsylvania, hometown folks flocked to watch her pace her mile one last time.[226]

---

226 "Skeeter W. to Retire to Stock Farm", *Steuben Farmer's Advocate*, October 8, 1930, fultonhistory.com

VERSO OF PHOTO SAYS "ON THE WAY TO THE SYRACUSE FAIR." FROM LEFT, WILLARD & MARJORIE WOOD DOAN, CLINTON OR DEAN WOOD, UNKNOWN WOMAN, BERTHA DANIELS WOOD. FROM BACK, PERRY WOOD HOLDING CHILD OF WILLARD AND MARJORIE. (COURTESY MARYON PAINTER SWANSON.)

"SKEETER W." TO RETIRE TO STOCK FARM

—Picture from Sunday Telegram.

"SKEETER W" WITH MR. AND MRS. C. A. DURNIAN

The Advocate herewith presents the picture of "Skeeter W" a horse popular throughout the Southern Tier, as taken at the Steuben County Fair a few days ago. "Skeeter," born at Knoxville, Pa., was trained and originally owned by John Wakely of that place. She later was the property of the Bath Quartette Stables, and for five consecutive years raced through the Grand Circuit, her triumphs being many. Two years ago, the horse became property of W. Yelland, Frankford, Pa., a prominent turfman, and he has arranged for "Skeeter" to retire to a life of ease and comfort on the Yelland stock farm near Philadelphia.

"Skeeter" won her first race on the Bath track in 1921, and strangely, concluded her brilliant racing career on the same track, being in the free-for-all at the fair, Friday, Sept. 26th. Mrs. C. A. Durnian of Bath, who is shown with her husband and "Skeeter" in the picture, had the honor of driving "Skeeter" for the last time, when in racing trim, this being done by Mrs. Durnian on the Bath track, Saturday of Fair week. Mr. Yelland was a guest of Mr. and Mrs. Durnian during his stay in Bath.

1930 STEUBEN FARMER'S ADVOCATE, BATH, NEW YORK.

The following year when Skeeter gave birth to her first foal, the *Steuben Farmer's Advocate* ran a glowing announcement worthy of any celebrity's baby book. The paper proudly proclaimed that she was now the mother of an "excellent bay colt" and that "Skeeter W. was one of the most phenomenal pacers that ever went round the grand circuit."[227] Folks back home, from Knoxville to Bath, knew their hometown girl had done well.

Ed Geers

This book would not be complete without a final mention of Ed Geers, who published his memoirs in 1904 and continued holding the reins until the seasoned age of seventy-four. In September of 1924, he was racing in Wheeling, West Virginia, when the mare he was driving lost her footing. He was jolted out of his sulky, hit the track surface, and died that evening without regaining consciousness.[228] He had prevailed as premier driver and trainer, and his life defined the harness era at its high point. His hands held the reins of dozens of the best horses during the golden days of harness racing, and among those were several descended from Wood's Hambletonian #572.

In those days there was no retirement. Whether it was riding the rails and driving racehorses or raking hay behind a team in the field, men kept to their daily occupations until they died. Some, like Thomas S. Flood, C. J. Hamlin, Frank Work, and R. J. Reynolds, died wealthy. The many farmers and horsemen who populated this

227 *Steuben Farmer's Advocate*, June 24, 1931.
228 L. G. Duffy, "In Memory of E.F. Geers", *Harness Horse*, January 22, 1936, mi-harness.net.

narrative just got by. Their wealth was in their land, their families, and the talents for which they were remembered.

∞

Outliers

Two men in this cast of characters defied attempts to package them neatly into the family storyline. O. H. Wood and his son-in-law, Jerome W. Hathaway, lived just outside the margins of the pious, temperate Wood clan. In a family where belief in God was synonymous with paying all of one's bills, staying out of court, and keeping a low profile in the eyes of the community, these fellows gave folks something to talk about. They, too, loved fast horses. They did not fit in with the rest of the family, but they were too interesting and too deeply entwined in horses to exclude.

Like many families, the Wood folks had affection for one another, did favors for each other, and lent money to each other, with the complications that arose from that. They also competed with and sometimes unabashedly used one another. The clan was an eclectic blend of cousins, friends, and alliances in business and in marriage. On the one hand, O. H.'s affinity for racing horses and racetrack people kept the Woods' name and their stallion in the buying public's eye. But his associates, his financial dealings, and incidents like the tiff he got into with Thomas Berry, occasionally drew attention to the family name that his brothers may have wished to avoid.

Like many of his contemporaries staking their claims in the mid-nineteenth century, O. H. was a wheeler-dealer in land, cattle, and horses. Some made fortunes; others just made a living. Buying, selling, timbering, building, dabbling in retail, he was ever reinventing himself to make his way. His earliest extant letter was a handwritten note to an uncle back in New Jersey during the last year of the Civil War. In February, 1864, O. H. penned from Knoxville about the price per head for cows and how many he could send on a boxcar to New Jersey. If he could not fill the car with cattle, he offered, he would top the load off with some horses to sell.[229]

As more of the horse stories unfolded in the records, the question shifted: which Wood man had really known the colt Dan's potential and set out to stand him? By the time of the author's childhood, family oral tradition had dwindled along the lines of: Father Oliver L. brought his three sons, O. H., Will, and Joseph when he decided to relocate to Deerfield for better farm land. The father brought the young stallion also and began his breeding career as soon as he arrived. He kept the horse and left him to Joseph when he died. Joseph continued the horse's career and made a nice sideline income with the horse breeding.

It was straightforward, with more pride than details. But a closer look at the circumstances begged for better answers. Why would a farmer past the age of sixty years who had been a dairy farmer and butter maker his whole life, spend money on a pedigreed colt and pack up for new territory not accessible by any near railroad? Oliver L. had followed his older sons, Absalom and O. H. But who really wanted the colt of Abdallah? Which one of these men knew of his breeding, his potential, and saw the opportunity for raising horses in Deerfield? It may have been O. H. who asked his father to buy the colt from VanSickle.

O. H.'s goal to stand a stud horse of his own had likely been frustrated by his family. In an early advertisement for the stallion

---

229 O. H. Wood to Asa Elston, New Jersey, February 26, 1864, private collection.

Dan in 1866, it was O. H. who placed the notice and seemed to be in control of the horse.[230] At some point, likely after mortgage foreclosure on various tracts of O. H.'s land, differences with him about his horsemen friends' use and handling of horses, and impacted by legal wrangling after O. H. sold their kinfolk note to David Billings—whom the Woods considered a usurer—father Oliver L. seemed to have concluded that the stallion Dan was better off in the hands of Will and Joseph.[231]

HAMBLETONIAN, Jr.—Sire, Hambletonian; grandsire, Abdallah; g-grandsire, old Mambrino; g-g-grandsire, imported Messenger.

Seven years old, 16 hands high, dark roan, can trot a mile in less than three minutes. He can show more good stock than any other stallion in Tioga county.

Will stand the ensuing season at the stable of the proprietor, in Knoxville, until August 1, '66.

For terms, see large posters.

Knoxville, May 16, 1866.   O. H. WOOD.

Wellsboro Agitator, June 20, 1866

O. H. remained optimistic. When his daughter, Sarah, married Jerome W. Hathaway (1847–1912) in 1870, O. H. gained an ally in his resilient, adventurous young son-in-law. Hathaway earned a living with various ventures and often returned to his usual occupation of running a hotel and livery stable. Hathaway had stints at both the

---

230 *Wellsboro Agitator*, June 20, 1866.
231 *Wood*, 1881.

Adams House hotel in Knoxville and also the Park Hotel in Tioga.[232] Livery stables were equivalent to a rental car agency and were usually located adjacent to an inn or hotel. The guy who ran the hotel and rented rigs to railway travelers had a pulse on who was going where and what business was going down. With Hathaway at his side, O. H. had yet a new horse partner.

No evidence was found that O. H. raced or registered his Wood's Guy Miller stallion with the association. Neither did he and Hathaway register Hathaway's Guy Miller. Though they catered to a lower-priced market, O. H. and Hathaway put their stallions out at stud in direct competition to the horse O. H. once handled, the horse who became the centerpiece of his two younger brothers' business. That O. H. was determined to stand a stud from the line of Rysdyk's horse was clear. His persistence with this line of horses seemed to answer the question of how the Woods got into the trotting stock business. The family did not fall into it by chance, O. H. had been the one who had first found the colt Dan and sought him out back in 1861.

---

232 "License Court", *Wellsboro Agitator*, February 13, 1907.

MYTHS DISPELLED

1. When you see the bronze statue of the famous trotting mare American Girl at Eldridge Park in Elmira, where she raced (and died on the track) in 1875, she is *not* closely related to any of the Wood horses. Wood horses did likely race at Eldridge Park and possibly competed against American Girl.

2. If you've heard someone say that Wood horses raced at Camptown, in Bradford County, Pennsylvania, where Stephen Foster was supposedly inspired to pen his folk tune "Camptown Races," no evidence was found connecting trotting horses with the Camptown races, as that track was primarily a running-horse track rather than a harness track.

3. When you see the statue of Man-o-War at Kentucky Horse Park or images of Dan Patch, neither was closely related to the Wood horses, though both shared some common bloodlines farther back.

4. When you see the iconic image of bearded old William Rysdyk with Hambletonian #10, you can know that he *is* the grandsire of Wood's Hambletonian. You can know how, where, when, and some of the why.

5. Why aren't there more pictures of the horses trotting? Kilburn Jim's life straddled the era between the lithograph and the photograph. Photography had not yet progressed to be able to capture an image of a moving subject, i.e., a horse in motion. So up until then, most of the horse races were chronicled by sketch or lithograph. The stereoptic image of Nancy Hackett is a blending of two images. It also bears heavy damage from having been fastened to a wall, perhaps with a tack in the middle. The photographs that do exist were of horses standing still to allow time for the lens to focus. It was well into the 1890s that newspapers began to have the capability to print photographs in their papers or capture the horse in motion.

6. A persistent tale cropping up in the Perry Wood branch told how, as a youngster, Perry was given the job of accompanying a horse to the Midwest on the train. Supposedly the trip took several days, and the boy was to care for the horse through to its destination, at which point he returned home by himself. Some time was spent attempting to corroborate the story with a print source, but no news archive account was found. These would have been the peak years—1885—when colts or mares may have been sold or bred and shipped to all points, many by railcar. It is a good story and plausible enough, just not documented in print.

7. There were across the nation harness racehorses who had the same names as several horses from the Woods, and could have become easily confused with Wood horses: Allegany Boy, Nancy Hackett, Nightingale, Jenny, Superior, etc. The

author has attempted to corroborate each horse featured in this narrative across multiple print sources, including the allbreeds pedigree database, to present information as accurately as possible.

8. One print source related a fascinating tale in which Oliver Wood's sons – O. H., Joseph, or William? – surreptitiously took the stallion to Cuba, New York, in 1871 and entered him with a teammate in a wagon race there. The story claimed that it was one of the only times the stallion was raced and that the team handily won the race. It continued that the "old man" was so distraught because of his piety and aversion to betting that he called a prayer meeting. Did he insist that his sons repent? Intriguing as it was, the tale could not be confirmed.[233]

---

233 J.J.Miller, "Wood's Hambletonian", *Wallace's Monthly*, v. XI, no. 4, April, 1885, 168, Hathitrust Digital Library.

LIST OF HORSES

Name	Sex	Date Foaled	Breeder	Last Known Owner	Location	Record, if any	Source
Achates#12763	stallion	1878	Joseph Wood	H. J. Skinner	Mckean County, PA		WTRv.9
Albert W.#10071	stallion	1884	Joseph Wood				WTRv.8
Allegany Boy#3401	stallion	1874	David Clark		Wellsboro, PA	2:27 1/4	WTRv.8
Allegany Girl	mare	1875	W.C. & J. Wood	W. Selkregg	Northeast, PA		
Ambler	gelding	1871	George H. Fitzwater	S.R. Clark	Elmira, NY	2.3	
Anna M.	mare						WY1890
Annetta	mare	1881	H.M. Davis		Vermont		WY1890
Argo A.#9172	stallion	1882	Joseph Wood	Ross Leach	Westfield, PA	2.28	WTRv.8
Argonaut	gelding	1872?	Joseph Wood	John Hounstein	Rochester, NY	2:23 1/4	Chester
Billy Ray	gelding		Nelson G. Ray			2.23 3/4	WTRv.6
Blossom	gelding		Joseph Wood	John Murphy			Chester
Blue Mare	mare		O. H. Wood	Dr. Daniel Curry	Hornellsville, NY	2:23	Chester
Bonnie Belle	mare	1879	H. S. Mathews	Guy Miller	Chester, NY		WTRv.6

Name	Sex	Date Foaled	Breeder	Last Known Owner	Location	Record, if any	Source
Bucephalus#14554	stallion	1877	Stephen Richards		Covington, PA	2:30	WTRv.10
Charley Van	gelding		R. M. Ketcham		Wellsboro, PA		WY1886
Chilcoot	stallion	1912	Walnut Hall Farm	Robert Bennett	Ontario, CAN	2.04 1/2	CHRHF
Chrystine	mare	1876	Jerome Barnhart			2.29 1/4	WYv.6
Col. Doty	gelding		M. D. VanScoter		Binghamton, NY		Chester
Cowanesque Chief#8238	stallion	1883	Jerome Hathaway	Jerome Hathaway	Elmira, NY		WTRv.7
Daniel Lee	stallion			Isaac Failing	Cuba, NY		newsarchive
Elda B.	mare	1880	W.C. & J. Wood			2.20 1/2	WYv.6
Fleetwood	Morgan x stallion			William Lanning	Woodhull, NY		newsarchive
Floodwood	stallion	1886	Thomas S. Flood		Elmira, NY		newsarchive
Flora Bassett	mare	1880?			St. Joseph, MO		WTRv.7
Frankie F.	mare	1878	Anson Holmes	Dr. Frank H. Flood	Elmira, NY		WTRv.5
Gilbert S.#10392	stallion	1885	Joseph Wood	C. Simmons	Borden, NY		WTRv.8
Hambletonian Dan, Jr.	stallion		Devilla A. Stowell	Devilla A. Stowell	Wellsboro, PA		newsarchive
Halwood	stallion			Erastus Maxson	Brookfield, NY		newsarchive
Harvester	stallion			Mr. Welch			WYv.4
Helen Ray	mare		James G. Wakely		Austinburg, PA		newsarchive

Name	Sex	Date Foaled	Breeder	Last Known Owner	Location	Record, if any	Source
Hengerer	stallion	1884	C. J. Hamlin		East Aurora, NY		farmcatalog
Hereward#8801	stallion	1887	C. J. Hamlin	J. McGuire	New York, NY		WTRv.7
Howard Jay	stallion	1876	George Strothoff		Burdett, NY	2.21 1/4	Chester
Humming Bird	mare	1874	J. G. Seely				WTRv.7
Independence	stallion						newsarchive
Ingomar	gelding	1874	Noah Everitt			2.23	Chester
Johnny B.#1783	stallion	1866	D. W. Boom	A.W.Smith	Cuba NY	2.38	WTRv.5
Kate Wood	mare	1879			Brookville PA		Chester
Keystone#2447	stallion	1875	Ira Carrier		Brookville PA		Chester
Kilburn Jim#571	stallion	1866	Jonas Kilburn	M. D. VanScoter	Hornellsville, NY	2.23	WTRv.4
Kilburn JimJr#4768	stallion		Fred Miller	Lawrence Hopper	Hornellsville, NY	2.21	
Kit Sanford	mare	1873	J.C. Bonham		Emporium PA	2.21 1/4	
Kitty Wood	mare	1871	F. H. Arnold			2.24 1/4	Chester
Lady Strang	mare		Frank Strang	O. H. Wood	Knoxville PA		WTRv.6
Major Wood#8596	stallion	1885	Thomas S. Flood	Thomas S. Flood	Elmira, NY		WTRv.7
Mamie Wood	mare	1884	Thomas S. Flood	R. J. Reynolds	Winston Salem NC	2.20 1/2	newsarchive
Maudie Bell	mare					2.46	WYv.6
Mayburn/Haldane	team geldings			Samuel F. Clark	Elmira, NY		newsarchive
Minnequa Maid	mare	1874	Joseph Wood	C. J. Hamlin	East Aurora, NY		newsarchive
Minta	mare	1885	J.B.Card		Sylvania PA		WTRv.7

Name	Sex	Date Foaled	Breeder	Last Known Owner	Location	Record, if any	Source
Meryl/Myrtie	pair brood mares		W.C. & J. Wood	C. J. Hamlin	East Aurora, NY		farmcatalog
Nancy Hackett	mare	1870	Elmer Hackett	W. C.& J. Wood	Utica NY	2.2	newsarchive
Nancy S.	mare			R. B. Carr			WYv.5
Nancy / Nellie Woods	team mares	1885/ 1884	Jacob Wainwright	T. A. Hollenbeck	Springboro PA		WTRv.7
Nightingale	mare	1885	C. J. Hamlin	C. J. Hamlin	East Aurora, NY	2.08	newsarchive
Nonpareil#9435	stallion	1986	J. W. Bigoney	Mr. Slayton	Conneautville, PA		WYv.6
Peter	gelding			Thomas S. Flood	Elmira, NY		WYv.3
Regina	mare	1878	Thomas S. Flood	Frank Work	New York, NY		newsarchive
Richard Schobell#0113	stallion	1877	Lott Bennett	Lott Bennett	Canaseraga, NY	2.12	WYv.7
Sam F.	gelding					2.26 3/4	WYv.4
Scapegoat	gelding, dual gaited	1892	C. J. Hamlin	George Castle	Chicago, IL	2.25 & 2.11 1/4(p)	WYvols.14,15
Skeeter W.	mare	1917	J. G. Wakely	Frank Yelland	Philadelphia, PA	2.03	newsarchive
Skyland Girl	mare	1893	H. H. Wilson Estate		Baltimore, MD	2.14 1/2	newsarchive
Spotted Sam	stallion	1878	John H. Leets			2.29 3/4	WYv.4
Superior, discrepancy	stallion	1879					newsarchive
Telephone	gelding	1877	A. Davidson		Williamsport, PA	2.22 1/2	WYv.21

Other horses sold as broodmares, found named in records or news archives but uncorroborated in race sources or which were not given names were not included here. For example, an early mare named Katie B. had no sanctioned race record and was sold to Theodore Cobb in Whitesville, New York. There she became a broodmare and the foundation of a line of fast mares at Cobb's stables from which J.G. Wakely's race mares produced Skeeter W. and Helen Ray. Richard Schobell was known by several names and became a prolific sire in western New York, as did Bucephalus in the southern part of Tioga County, PA. Their offspring were not listed here. WTR means Wallace's Trotting Register, WY means Wallace's Register.

BIBLIOGRAPHY

Atlas of Allegany County, New York. New York: D. G. Beers, 1869.

Atlas of Tioga County, Pennsylvania. New York: F. W. Beers, 1875.

Bradburn, John. *Breeding and Developing the Trotter*. Boston: American Horse Breeder Publishing Company, 1906, 27–28. Hathitrust Digital Library.

Busbey, Hamilton. *The Trotting and the Pacing Horse in America*. New York: Macmillan Company, 1904.

Chester, Walter T. *Chester's Complete Record of Trotting and Pacing, Containing Summaries of All Races Trotted or Paced in the United States or Canada, from the Earliest Dates to the Close of 1883*. New York: The Compiler, 1884. Google Books.

Geers, E. F. *Ed. Geers' Experience with the Trotters and Pacers*. Buffalo, NY: Matthews-Northrup, 1901.

Gocher, W. H. *Trotalong*. Hartford, CT: W. H. Gocher, 1928.

Groene, Bertram H. *Tracing Your Civil War Ancestor*. Winston-Salem, NC: John F. Blair, 1973.

Hakes, Hon. Harlo, et al. *Landmarks of Steuben County, New York*. Syracuse, NY: D. Mason, 1896.

Jerome, Robert D., and Wisbey, Herbert A. Jr., eds. *Mark Twain in Elmira*. Elmira, NY: Mark Twain Society, 1977.

Kemp, Harry C. *Kemp's Life Story*. New York: Carleton Press, 1960.

Leerhsen, Charles. *Crazy Good: The True Story of Dan Patch, the Most Famous Horse in America*. New York: Simon & Schuster, 2008.

McCarr, Ken. *The Kentucky Harness Horse*. Lexington, KY: University Press of Kentucky, 1978.

Meginness, John F., et al. *History of Tioga County, Pennsylvania*. Vols. 1 and 2. Philadelphia: R. C. Brown, 1897.

Pearson, John. *Blood Royal: The Story of the Spencers and the Royals*, New York: HarperCollins, 1999.

Pierce, Geneva Griffin. *The Romance of a Changing Life*. Westfield, PA: Valley Dollar Saver, 1970.

Reeves, J. H. *The Orange County Stud Book*. New York: Jason H. Tuttle, 1880. Hathitrust Digital Library.

Sanders, J. H. *Horse Breeding: Being the General Principles of Heredity Applied to the Business of Breeding Horses, with Instructions for the Management of Stallions, Brood Mares and Young Foals, and the Selection of Breeding Stock*. Chicago: J. H. Sanders, 1888. Hathitrust Digital Library.

Sandow, Robert M. *Deserter Country: Civil War Opposition in the Pennsylvania Appalachians* New York: Fordham University Press, 2009.

Sexton, John L. *History of Tioga County, PA, with Illustrations, Portraits, & Sketches, etc.* New York: W. W. Munsell, Press of George MacNamara, 1883.

Stiles, T. J. *The First Tycoon: The Epic Life of Cornelius Vanderbilt.* New York: Vintage Books, 2010.

Taber, Thomas T. III. *Logging Railroad Era of Lumbering in Pennsylvania.* Vols. 4 and 7. Williamsport, PA: Thomas T. Taber, 1972, 1975.

Towner, Ausburn. *A History of the Valley and County of Chemung.* Syracuse, NY: D. Mason, 1892.

Wallace, John Hankins. *Wallace's Year-book of Trotting and Pacing.* New York: Wallace Trotting Register Company, Vols. 4–22, 1875–1902. Hathitrust Digital Library.

Ward, Geoffrey C., and Duncan, Dayton. *Mark Twain.* New York: Alfred A. Knopf, 2001.

Wood, F. J. "Sketch of Life of Oliver Livingston Wood." Unpublished, March 24, 1965. Private collection of Mary Wood Wetmore.

THE AUTHOR

Ellen Williams has a B.A. in history from Clarion University, and has worked as a legal abstractor and a librarian in a variety of settings. During her time as director at Knoxville Public Library, she facilitated for several years a popular winter local history roundtable series on topics such as the Civil War, tobacco culture, the lumber industry, agriculture and railroads in the Cowanesque Valley region. Inspired by the Pulitzer Prize-winning work of Laurel Thatcher Ulrich, her favorite projects are the interpretation and transcription of vintage diaries. Her first horse as a youngster was a Standardbred mare retired from the race track. The author is a 5th-generation descendant of Oliver L. Wood, and has lived much of her life within view of the barn where the stallion lived.